DECORATING
with
TILE

DECORATING
with
TILE

Margaret Sabo Wills

CREATIVE HOMEOWNER®, Upper Saddle River, New Jersey

Editorial Director: Timothy O. Bakke
Art Director: W. David Houser
Production Manager: Stanley Podufalski

Editor: Carolyn Anderson-Feighner
Copy Editor: Ellie Sweeney
Proofreader: Stanley Sudol
Photo Editing: Carolyn Anderson-Feighner
Photo Research: Amla Sanghvi, Stanley Sudol
Indexer: schroederindexing.com

Book Designer: Mary Zisk
Assistant Graphic Designer: Robert Strauch
Front Cover Design: Scott Molenaro
Front Cover Photography: Mark Lohman
Back Cover Design: Mary Zisk
Back Cover Photography (clockwise):
Jessie Walker, Mark Lohman, davidduncanlivingston.com
Manufactured in the United States of America

Current Printing (last digit)
10 9 8 7 6 5 4 3 2

Decorating with Tile, First Edition
Library of Congress Catalog Card Number: 00-105444
ISBN: 1-58011-029-0

CREATIVE HOMEOWNER PRESS®
A Division of Federal Marketing Corp.
24 Park Way, Upper Saddle River, NJ 07458
Web site: **www.creativehomeowner.com**

DEDICATION

For my mother and father, my siblings, my in-laws, my dazzling children,

Benedict and Rosalind, and, most of all, for my husband, Stewart, my

fellow voyager, my dearest love, who makes all things possible.

ACKNOWLEDGMENTS

To all the professionals in the field who shared their knowledge of

ceramic tile so freely, including the inspiring and helpful

Joseph Taylor of Tile Heritage Foundation and David Malkin at Tile Source Inc.,

who provided historical information. For general information on today's

products, I'm indebted to such industry organizations as Tile Council of

America, Italian Tile Center at the Italian Trade Commission, Tiles of

Spain at the Trade Commission of Spain, and the Tile Promotion Board.

Thanks also to tile makers Peter King of Stonehaus, Genevieve Sylvia of

Pewabic Pottery, Nawal Motawi at Motawi Tile, and Frank Giorgini of Udu

Drum, and interior designers Beverly Ellsley, Deborah Habicht, and

Christopher Drake. For actually getting this book on the shelves,

accolades go to my editor, Carolyn Anderson-Feighner.

And for getting the book "off" the shelves, thank you to my readers.

CONTENTS

Introduction

Over the centuries, ceramic tile has proved itself a delightfully versatile decorating tool. In ceramic tile, a raw material literally common as dirt becomes both a utilitarian surface and a soaring art form—sleekly modern or quaintly rustic, laden with history or truly one-of-a-kind. Perhaps because it's born of earth, water, air, and fire, tile retains a simple, elemental appeal, even in its most ornate or high-tech incarnations. With the pleasing repetition of its grid, the intricacy of its decorations, and its tactile, light-catching surface, tile lends a sense of texture and human scale whenever it becomes part of the architecture.

On a less-exalted note, ceramic technology has been borrowed and stolen among cultures all through history because ceramic surfaces are wonderfully practical—durable, hygienic, and resistant to fading, warping, burning, and moisture. These advantages prompted ancient peoples to craft pots and to sheathe buildings in ceramics. In our own time, ceramic tile has even followed to the outer edge of the human experience, serving as the heat shields for our spacecraft, bearing up to the inferno of reentry.

This book intends to be—just like tile itself—beautiful and useful. In these pages, we'll present an overview of ceramic tile's vivid history, from its old-world roots to its latest blossoming in our own era, perhaps providing a few ideas along the way for the homeowner seeking a period flavor. Separate chapters will examine the dazzling variety of tiles available to you, both from large commercial sources and the burgeoning number of tile artists and small studios, along with practical pointers on choosing products for specific purposes. After a look at how some basic decorating principles are played out in tile, we'll turn to special concerns connected with using tile in kitchens and baths as well as in less-expected settings.

Throughout, we'll celebrate tile's decorative potential. Designing with tile involves not only selecting the individual units from an inspiring range of decorative choices but also composing the overall picture. Even the plainest off-the-shelf products can be combined with fresh imagination. On these pages, we aim to show an array of products and decorating approaches—from quiet and classic looks with wide appeal to the most off-beat and idiosyncratic—to illustrate the modern range of this ancient material.

Opposite: Tile has a pleasing visual rhythm played up in high-contrast checks.
Above left: A Moravian Pottery tile with a design etched in a translucent glaze shows the decorative potential of a single square.
Above right: Spain's fourteenth-century Alhambra Palace shows tile brought together in dazzling patterns.

CHAPTER I

A BRIEF HISTORY OF TILE

Old World Roots

Tile is a cosmopolitan material with a saga spanning continents and centuries. Ceramics that are thousands of years old still survive to tell their stories, long after other artistic traces have crumbled. Tile employs the methods and materials of pottery, one of our oldest forms of technology. The same rivers that fostered the first cities also laid deposits of workable clay.

"When someone first fired a clay pot," muses ceramist Peter King, "it was the first time we deliberately changed our world at the molecular level."

Though pottery was the stuff of everyday life from early on, tile has flourished only under certain conditions: when an empire was in the making, with settled cities, lively trade, and enough patrons—aristocratic, religious, or just plain well-heeled—to support the infrastructure of kilns and specialized craftspeople. When times turned bad, those same craftspeople carried their skills with them and followed rumors of better markets elsewhere. Thus tile's artistic lineage is an international hopscotch, as ceramic techniques and decorative ideas were stolen, borrowed, adapted, abandoned, and revived.

ANCIENT EMBELLISHMENTS

Clay was a natural early building material—brick was invented independently in several early cultures, as humans learned, in effect, to "make stones." Clay designates a wide range of natural substances, formed when rocks, such as granite and gneiss, weather and decompose.

When wet, clay's disklike microscopic particles slide easily across each other. But as they dry, they interlock into a rigid matrix, which firing at high temperatures renders permanent.

A *primary* clay is dug where it was first formed and is a pure, fine-grain substance, such as the white kaolin used in Chinese porcelain. More common *secondary* clays are transported by water and redeposited, mixed with minerals and impurities that add different working qualities and various colors, such as a terra-cotta red indicating the presence of iron.

When our Neolithic ancestors gathered in closely spaced houses of mud-brick some 9,000 years ago in what is now Turkey, they were already embellishing the plain clay surfaces with relief patterns and enigmatic painted murals.

In the fourth millennium B.C., Egyptians dressed ceremonial buildings with fired slabs glazed in blue copper and decorated with colored enamels.

Ancient Mesopotamian cities were fronted with unglazed terra-cotta and colorful architectural ceramics. Thrifty builders stacked softer sun-baked clay blocks inside, protected with a covering of costlier fired and sometimes decorated brick. Brilliantly glazed animals paraded on Babylon's famous Ishtar Gate, built about 580 B.C. by Nebuchadnezzar II, along with a modest inscription, echoed in the hearts of city planners through the ages: "I set up wild bulls and furious dragons in front of the gates, thus magnificently adorned with

Above: The ancient Romans achieved subtle tonal effects in their mosaic artworks.
Previous pages: A close-up from Portugal's Estoi Palace shows the exuberant blue-and-white tilework that the country has loved since the sixteenth century.

luxurious splendor for all mankind to look at in surprise."

Ancient Greeks and Romans built their monuments in stone; architecturally, ceramics served for workaday floors, roofs, and drains. The classical world and the ensuing Byzantine Empire of the early Christians, however, did excel in intricate, expressive mosaics, catching the light in textured surfaces of stone, glass, and sometimes tile.

Above: Opulent tiled roofs, glazed in vivid reds and yellows and carved in high relief, add to the splendor of The Forbidden City, Beijing, China. **Left:** Ravenna, Italy's Church of San Vitale, completed in A.D. 547 glows with the light-catching texture of Byzantine mosaics.

From antiquity, eastern Asia produced sophisticated ceramics, but early architectural use was limited to heavily glazed roof tiles, and plaques and deep-relief wall tiles for royal palaces and tombs. Fine Chinese porcelains, however, coveted all along the ancient trade routes, helped spark the Middle East's dazzling tilework between the seventh and seventeenth centuries.

ISLAMIC ARTISTRY

As the Islamic faith spread from Arabia across the Middle East and North Africa from the seventh century onward, it invigorated a variety of ceramic traditions, such as the rich artistry of the former Persia, present-day Iran. By the end of the thirteenth century, mosques and secular buildings across the region were lavishly tiled, inside and out. Later, the center of production shifted to what is now the city of Iznik, in present-day Turkey, under the patronage of the Ottoman sultans. Moorish conquerors carried Islamic tile making into Spain.

Because Islamic teachings forbid human images and discourage the opulent ornamentation of gold and jewels, ceramics became a prized artistic medium. In gleaming ceramics, Islamic

Above: Because their religious tenets forbid human images, Islamic tile makers intrigue the eye with intricate, abstract designs in dazzling hues.

Above: A Samarkand cuerda seca stellar tile, circa 1450.
Below: Moorish tile swirls throughout Spain's fourteenth-century Alhambra Palace.

potters covered walls, niches, minarets, and fountains with interlocking scrolls and arabesques, stylized florals, and flowing Arabic script. The broad palette emphasized vivid blues and turquoise, and, later, a "sealing-wax" red. Vivid, solid-color glazed tiles were also painstakingly cut and reassembled into large-scale mosaics that still shine today in the courtyards of Spain's fourteenth-century Alhambra Palace.

To achieve bold, mosaiclike contrasts on individual tiles, Moorish tile makers contained the pooled glazes with fine string impregnated with grease and manganese. This "resist" line burned off in the firing to leave a bold black outline, a technique called *cuerda seca,* or "dry cord." *Cuenca,* or "bowl," patterns similarly separate the glazes with the ridges of a stamped, high-relief design.

Medieval Islamic potters also discovered that tin oxide added to a basic lead glaze created a creamy, opaque ground. Not only did this tin glaze make the red or pink clays as white as coveted Chinese porcelains but it held painted decoration in place without heavy

lines and ridges during the firing. Metallic oxides—cobalt for blue, manganese for purple, copper for green, antimony for yellow—could be brushed on and rendered brilliant in reaction to the kiln's heat. Or fired at a lower temperature in an air-starved *reducing* kiln, the oxides would fuse into the metallic sheen of lusterware.

MEDIEVAL MAJESTY

European Crusaders in the Middle Ages brought back reports of such tiled splendors. Closer to home was a different decorative influence: the grand mosaic pavements left from former Roman outposts across Europe. So when lavish cathedrals arose, from the eleventh to the fifteenth centuries, tile was used just as in the mosques of the Middle East, in architecture designed to inspire awe.

While Islamic tile was vibrantly glazed and intricately patterned to gleam on walls and towers in the desert sunlight, Europe's medieval tilework created richly patterned floors in earthy tones. It conveyed a quiet, massive grandeur within soaring interiors, illuminated with stained glass and candlelight. In twelfth-century France, Cistercian monks laboriously cut and assembled geometrical tile in radiating patterns for cathedral and abbey floors and carried the practice to England as part of the Gothic style. Eventually, as these overall patterns became simpler and less labor-intensive, the individual tiles became more decorative, with geometric motifs, heraldic symbols, and stylized figures, natural or fantastical.

Instead of bright glazes, early European tiles were decorated with a contrasting *slip,* or liquefied clay. For *sgraffito* designs, the tile body was covered in light slip, which was selectively scratched away to reveal the darker clay underneath. Or the slip was poured into the indentations of a stamped design, shaved flat, and fired to *burn in* the contrasting pattern of an *encaustic* square, a basic element of Gothic style until the early sixteenth century.

In the sixteenth century, the Reformation led to the disbanding of monasteries, and European tastes turned toward

Opposite: Islamic tile achieves its impact both through geometric puzzles of pure color and individual tiles covered in complex scrolls and arabesques.

Top: A thirteenth-century floor in Yorkshire's Rievaulx Abbey shows the soft, earthy tones of early European tile. **Above:** An early Anglo-Saxon tile excavated at York's All Saints Church bears a stamped design.

By adding tin-oxide to a basic lead glaze, medieval Islamic potters could give ceramics a creamy white face, ideal for added decoration. Across Europe in the succeeding centuries, tile artisans adopted and adapted the glazing technique.

Left: Dutch workshops in the seventeenth century produced cheerful, simple motifs such as this colorful tulip. **Right:** Inspired by Chinese import wares, this blue-on-white floral panel in John Knox's House, Edinburgh, is eighteenth-century Dutch. **Below:** Spanish tile makers inclined toward multihued, painterly designs.

stylish tin-glazed tile introduced throughout Spain and Italy. Since the mid-1400s, Italy's colorful pottery and tile had reflected the lushness of Renaissance painting. Portugal came late to tin glazing, but by the mid-sixteenth century its fountains, courtyards, and entire building facades were ceramic clad.

From Italy, production of tin-glazed wares spread to France, Germany, and the Netherlands, often under the guidance of expatriate Italian craftsmen. The products themselves traveled under names taken from their major trading centers:

majolica or *maiolica* for Majorca, Spain; *faience,* for the Italian port of Faenza; and, later, *delftware* for the Dutch city of Delft.

Italians used tiles underfoot, while Britons favored them for floors and fireplaces. German and Austrian households centered on big heating stoves called *smuigers,* clad with tiles figured in green, brown, and yellow. The Dutch, perhaps influenced by years under Spanish rule, applied tile liberally to walls, windowsills, fireplaces, and baseboards. The sturdy white tiles maximized the cool, gray sunlight entering the windows, and unlike flaky white-wash, bore up to the soggy climate.

By the seventeenth century, the Dutch dominated tin-glazed tile production with efficient workshops of artisans hand-painting patterns over *pounced* outlines, applied with powdered graphite on pricked-paper stencils. The craze for Chinese porcelain helped make blue-on-white the preferred scheme.

Widely exported, Dutch tiles were designed not just for majestic estates but for cheerful homes of an emerging middle class. The charming designs, realistically and lightly drawn, included landscapes and sailing ships, flowers and soldiers, biblical scenes, and children at play. Small corner motifs sometimes provided a visual link in a wall of assorted patterns. The English, often aided by transplanted Dutch artisans, started producing their own popular delft-ware, in the eighteenth century, in London, Liverpool, and Bristol. The eighteenth century also gave rise to England's Potteries District in Stoke-on-Trent, Staffordshire, the home of such famous potteries as Wedgwood, Spode, Minton, and Maw & Company.

INDUSTRIALIZATION AND PROLIFERATION

In 1756 John Sadler and Guy Green, two Liverpool printers, signed an affidavit stating that they "did within the space of six hours…print upwards of twelve hundred earthenware tiles…more in number and better, and neater than one hundred skilful pot painters could have painted."

For that reason, printed *transferware* became the norm for decorative tile production in the following century. A highly detailed, multicolored design could be stamped with oxides on a transfer paper, and pressed onto a fired tile. The paper was soaked off, and the design, sometimes with some additional hand-painting, was protectively glazed and sealed with a second firing.

Yet tiles themselves were still laboriously handmade of moist clay, prone to warping and cracking during drying and firing. (Much tile history has been garnered from factory dumps of flawed tiles.)

Beginning in 1828, second-generation tile maker Herbert Minton began studying medieval tiles and took a share in a patent to re-create the lost art of encaustic designs. Throughout years of experimentation, he overcame the

Below: British tile production boomed in the nineteenth century as new production methods made precise designs easily repeatable and thus more affordable. This Minton tile was designed by A.W.N. Pugin from his "Floreated Ornament," 1849.

Above: Filling in a stamped design with a contrasting clay created durable "encaustic" tile, a staple of Victorian public buildings and churches. This Minton inlaid floor tile was used in Temple Church, London, in 1849.

technical difficulties of drying and firing two different clays as a cohesive whole. By the 1840s Minton's encaustic squares were a company staple.

When another patent was granted in 1840 for making buttons by ramming almost-dry powdered clay into dies under high pressure, Minton bought in immediately. He saw the potential for tile making: Dust-pressed tiles were smooth, precise, predictable products, perhaps already stamped with a dimensional design, ready for glazing and firing without lengthy drying. When transfer-printing combined with dust-pressed bodies, British production soared in the latter nineteenth century as tiles became affordable.

Ceramics fit perfectly with the eclectic, visually lush, high-spirited decorating of the Victorian era. In the 1850s and 1860s, in a glow of national pride, the British revived medieval Gothic designs as the dignified, proper style for churches and public buildings, where encaustic tiles were *de rigueur*. Other historic revivals followed and overlapped—a fashionable house might have a dainty neoclassical bedroom, a staid Gothic library and an exotic Moorish parlor. Owen Jones's influential *The Grammar of Ornament*, published in 1856, presented color plates of historical decorative motifs meant to serve as inspirations, though manufacturers often lifted the designs in toto.

Tile production kept pace with Britain's unprecedented building boom. Ceramic seemed the modern, sanitary material for overcrowded cities, full of new kinds of buildings—train stations, factories, office complexes, government facilities, public baths, libraries, and new and restored churches. Just as in Nebuchadnezzar's day, public buildings dazzled the viewer with tile. On a smaller scale, a fishmonger's shop might boast tiled murals of leaping trout; a butcher's, grazing cows. Children's hospitals in Britain were cheered with tiled panels of fairy tales and historical vignettes.

Domestically, tile fashioned the intricately patterned entryways of new town houses, and the utilitarian kitchens, where a sternly lettered tile might exhort the servants to "Waste Not, Want Not." Fashionable fireplaces were flanked by thematic sets of tiles, perhaps depicting the seasons, a garden of flowers, romantic novels, or scenes from Shakespeare's plays.

THE CRAFTSMAN'S ART

The ascendance of the machine in tile making didn't pass without comment. In reaction, the most eloquent spokesperson was William Morris, an influential thinker and manufacturer. As the leading light of the Arts and Crafts philosophy, he called for a return to the integrity of

handcraftsmanship, and the fashioning of "honest" artworks for everyday use. Instead of trans-ferware's ornate, often highly realistic patterns, he envisioned designs that respected the limits of the tile surface, with clear, stylized, and flat images, which often reflected medieval or aus-tere Japanese inspirations.

Morris's own firm produced tile but with some technical troubles. A better exemplar of the artist/craftsman was Morris's associate, William De Morgan. The son of a chemist, De Morgan combined a technical grasp of glazes and clays with a brilliant artistic eye. He admired Islamic lusterware techniques and intricate patterns—one of his early triumphs was "Iznik" tile to complete a manor-house room of antique Middle Eastern ceramics. But his more than 1,000 tile designs ranged from delicate, stylized florals, bold medieval motifs, dense abstract patterns, and fantastical "beasties."

Morris tried hard to reconcile his idealization of the salt-of-the-earth craftsman with the resulting handmade products affordable only by the elite—products from De Morgan's work-

Above: An exemplar of Arts and Crafts tile production, William De Morgan covered this 1880s fireplace in Spring Bank House, Leeds, England, with medieval-inspired "beasties" in a red luster glaze.

shop were triple the cost of tiles by large commercial firms. But Britain's Arts and Crafts movement, much discussed in the newly available mass media, made it stylish to pursue aesthetic ideals. An eager marketplace eventually helped forge some alliance between craft and commerce. Manufacturers from the late 1800s onward produced fashionable art tiles, often involving some handwork, and certainly inspired by Arts and Crafts ideals. Designers within the movement, such as Charles F.A. Voysey and Walter Crane, also provided designs for commercial potteries.

While transfer-printing produced much of the nineteenth century's decorative tiles, many small workshops kept hand-crafted techniques alive, as did the studio departments of larger tile manufacturers. Tile historian Julian Barnard cites a wide-ranging Maw & Co. catalog of the era offering "Majolica and Enameled Tiles, white and variously tinted glazed Tiles, Decorated Glazed and Hand Painted Art Tiles, Glazed Encaustic, Incised, Enameled, Pate-sur-Pate [a cameolike effect with painted slip], Lustred and Gilt Tiles, Architectural Enrichments, etc." George Maw's interest in botany, archeology, and geology even resulted in tiles decorated with images of fossil tree roots and trilobites.

TURNING THE CENTURY

The Arts and Crafts' emphasis on beauty, distinctive surfaces, and exotic inspirations set the stage for Europe's turn-of-the-century Art Nouveau styles. The tactile, light-catching quality of glaze and the geometry of the tile grid worked compellingly with Art Nouveau's lush, shimmering hues; sinuous "whiplash" curves; and romantic themes.

Spanish architect Antonio Gaudí blended Art Nouveau into his own idiosyncratic vision with free-form mosaics of broken ceramics that covered equally free-form parks and apartment buildings in Barcelona and elsewhere.

Art Nouveau, never widely produced, didn't outlast the World War I, but transmuted into sleeker, and more easily

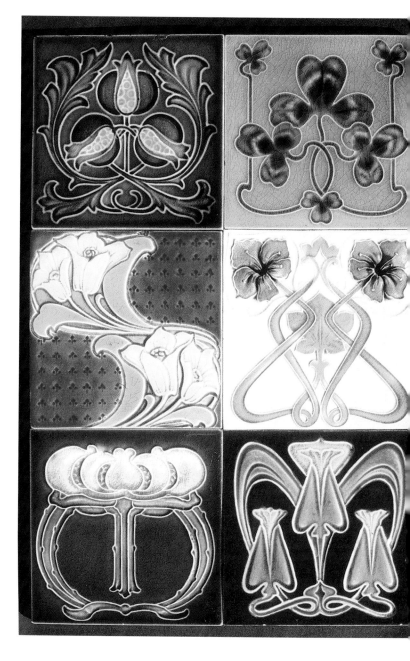

Left: A hand-painted William De Morgan tile exemplifies stylized Arts and Crafts design.
Below: Six English Art Nouveau tiles shine with the style's bright floral colors and sinuous curves.

manufactured Art Deco designs, which turned more elegantly geometric through the 1920s and the 1930s.

The Arts and Crafts movement, in its more rugged, socially idealistic aspects, also helped foster the stripped-down modernism of the twentieth century. Such minimalism was shaped in the Bauhaus, the influential German design school founded in 1919, with the goal of merging the fine and practical arts. But by the time the Nazis closed the school in 1933, the ceramics department was already dismantled, and the school was espousing a more functional philosophy of bold, strictly unornamented architecture. As its charismatic faculty scattered to architectural schools elsewhere, modernistic ideas were widely disseminated.

World events helped the International Style take root: the lean times of the 1930s, the austerity of the World War II era, and the need for rapid rebuilding after the war—all steered architectural style away from extravagance. Tile was looked upon as a serviceable material rather than sensual medium. It took a resurgence of interest in crafts in recent decades to bring tile back to its artistic heights.

Above: In his own imaginative version of Art Nouveau, Spanish architect Antonio Gaudí covered the winding benches of Barcelona's Park Güell with high-spirited broken-tile mosaics.

CHAPTER 2

TILE IN AMERICA

Roots and Blossoms

Though tile was imported to America from Colonial times onward, its domestic tile industry was late in blooming. By the early nineteenth century, several commercial potteries were producing household wares. Yet despite a few sporadic efforts (such as some flag-bedecked squares fired by a Vermont pottery for an 1853 trade fair), tile remained largely an imported luxury. The expansive floors of the Capitol, constructed in 1855, were paved with fine encaustic tiles—from Britain. It would be over 20 years before the birth of America's native tile industry.

STIRRINGS

Perhaps the biggest boost for America's fledgling tile industry was the 1876 Centennial Exposition in Philadelphia. This much-written-about outpouring of national pride, with 75 acres of exhibits, was attended by almost one-quarter of the population. There, Britain's leading tile manufacturers lavishly displayed their most fashionable products. They little reckoned how such showmanship would inspire America's own tile makers, both its visionary artists and hard-nosed businesspeople. The timing was right: with the Civil War and Reconstruction well behind them, Americans were devoting their attention and new prosperity to domestic comfort. Following the British fashion, tile had become desirable for the tastefully furnished home. Within a few years, tile factories had sprung up in Massachusetts, New York, New Jersey, Pennsylvania, Ohio, and Indiana, usually near clay deposits and transportation centers.

Above: For the mid-1980s renovation of the Capitol, the reproduction encaustic tiles were made by England's H&R Johnson to closely match the imported originals. **Previous pages:** When the Capitol's lavish floors were originally laid in the 1850s, America's own tile industry had not yet been born.

Britain also contributed an Arts and Crafts philosophy, which fostered a romantic regard for the artisan's handiwork, and an "Aesthetic" sensibility, championing the refining influence of beauty in everyday life, and "art for art's sake."

The burgeoning popular press, new libraries, and lecture circuits discussed such ideas for an expanding, urbanized middle class eager to pursue Beauty—handcrafted if their budgets allowed, or if not, some reasonable facsimile. American tastes inclined away from the precisely detailed transfer-printed tiles of earlier British tradition toward the sculpted, handmade look of Britain's "art tile." Many of the early art tiles of the 1880s and 1890s, though they might entail considerable hand-labor, tended to be dust-pressed with translucent, glossy glazes that ran and puddled over high-relief and incised *intaglio* designs, giving the single color a rich variety.

One visitor to the exposition was John Gardner Low, an apprentice to a Scottish potter in Massachusetts. In 1877, with financial backing from his father, also named John, he founded one of the most innovative early firms, the J. & J.G. Low Art Tile Works. "Low was on the leading edge," explains Joseph Taylor, president of the Tile Heritage Society, a nonprofit organization for the study and preservation of vintage tile. "No one was doing what his company was, or so well—his designs helped create the distinctively American tile." Low's designs, molded in precise relief, included delicate classical figures, natural scenes, and realistic portrait tiles (including a series of American presidents). For his patented "natural process" tiles, he laid actual leaves, grasses, and ferns on "green" unfired tiles, which were pressed to gain the precise, one-of-kind imprint.

Above and right: From the pioneering Low Art Tile Works, two 1882 "plastic sketches" by artist Arthur Osborne, render a Normandy street scene and a shepherd in fine dimensional detail covered in a glossy glaze.

Above: Pools and highlights of the translucent glaze play up the precise dust-pressed designs of these presidential portraits from Low Art Tile.

WORK OF MANY HANDS

Around the turn of the century, a bevy of individualistic tile makers hewed even closer to Arts and Crafts ideals, working by hand with temperamental malleable clays, covering the idio-syncratic, more roughly hewn designs with rich matte glazes.

One of the most influential of these was Harvard-educated Henry Chapman Mercer, who was born into a wealthy Pennsylvania family. After studying law and pursuing a successful archeology career, he founded the Moravian Pottery and Tile Works in 1898 on his Doylestown estate, where he eventually built Fonthill, his Gothic-inspired home. He also built a poured-concrete structure, styled on California's Spanish missions, to hold his workshops. There, artisans hand-pressed clay into molds, which had been cast from individually carved tiles. Mercer cast a wide net for design ideas, borrowing motifs from medieval, Gothic, Colonial and Pre-Columbian cultures. All shared a bold simplicity, molded in high relief and enhanced by rugged, highly varied glazes.

MORAVIAN POTTERY

Henry Chapman Mercer turned a scholarly passion for pre-industrial tools into a profitable business: the Moravian Pottery and Tile Works, inspired by the ceramics of German settlers. His handmade tiles made him a leader in America's turn-of-the-century Arts and Crafts movement.

Clockwise from above: Moravian Pottery's designs included a stylized dragonfly, a Craftsman-style Boston harbor scene, a dainty swan, and Colonial cornstalks.

Mercer's work strongly influenced Boston tile maker William Grueby, who had apprenticed for ten years, from age 13, at Low Art Tile. Grueby Faience Company, founded in 1894, was particularly known for its tube-lined and *cuenca*-molded designs, with piped-on or pressed ridges of clay to separate contrasting colors of the rich matte glazes he helped to popularize.

From the start, the Midwest was a stronghold for artistic tile makers, such as Cincinnati's prolific Rookwood Pottery, founded in 1880 by Maria Longworth Nichols. The pottery initiated tile making around 1901. Its high-relief designs with lush, satiny "vellum" glazes appeared in civic buildings, prestigious Eastern hotels, and New York City subway stations.

In the 1890s Horace Caulkins, a Midwest dental-supply manufacturer, invented the kerosene-powered Revelation kiln, capable of unprecedented temperatures. He then hired ceramist Mary Chase Perry (Stratton) to promote it to potteries throughout the east. In 1902, with a solid understanding of the competition and current ceramic technology, she and Caulkins founded the Detroit-based Pewabic Pottery, a firm especially esteemed for its deep, lustrous glazes in greens, purples, and golds.

Above left: The perfect topping for a turn-of-the-century Stickley oak table, a dozen tiles by Grueby Faience glow with the firm's variegated matte glaze.
Top right: A sailing ship from the Grueby workshops combines the characteristic glazes with a romantic image.
Above right: The Midwest's Rookwood Pottery showcases its hallmark satin finishes in a 1920 landscape panel.

Above left and right: Tiles by California tile maker Ernest Batchelder, circa the 1910s and 1920s, were hand-pressed in molds to create such fanciful low-relief images as a Gothic knight and an equally romanticized West Coast landscape. Hand-rubbed slip-glazes give them a subtle, mottled finish.

FROM CALIFORNIA CLAYS

California's decorative tile production didn't bloom until its population did, after the twentieth century's first decade. The West Coast operated under a separate set of ceramic influences: the earthy traditions of rough terra-cottas and adobes of Native Americans combined with the glowing colors and Islamic patterns of its Spanish heritage.

A giant of California's handcrafted tile was Ernest Batchelder, a transplanted easterner. He was already a successful design teacher by 1910, when he started to make ceramics in his backyard (perhaps inspired by his own home's Moravian tile fireplace). He soon outgrew this workshop. At the height of production in the mid-1920s, Batchelder employed up to 175 people in a factory near downtown Los Angeles. Batchelder's tiles were hand-pressed in low relief in plaster molds, with designs ranging from stylized medieval and Gothic animals and flowers to California scenery. Instead of glazing his tiles, he covered them with tinted, liquefied clays and then hand-rubbed them for a soft, mottled glow.

Similarly tinted and textured products depicting specific, romanticized scenes from the coastline, Yosemite, and the California missions were produced by Los Angeles's Claycraft Potteries—founded by the grandson of the Scottish potter who had taught J.G. Low two generations earlier.

California China Products Company, just south of San Diego, produced tile for the town's Santa Fe Railroad depot and for the 1915 Panama-California International Exposition. It

Left: In a massive hearth, the mellow hues and handmade look of Batchelder tiles capture the essence of a 1910 California Craftsman bungalow.

Top and above: Claycraft Potteries in Los Angeles captured Yosemite's Vernal Falls and El Capitan in fine detail, with the added depth of a lustrous glaze.

Opposite: In a sunlit hallway of the Adamson House tile museum, a lavish "rug" of 1920s Malibu tile reflects the colorful Moorish design approach born of California's Spanish heritage.

Right and below: California Faience, one of the larger northern California potteries, produced these round flower-decked "tea tiles," displaying the firm's skill in rendering fanciful, stylized designs.

launched another breed of California tiles: a vivid reinterpretation of Spanish and Mexican ceramic traditions. In contrast to the forest greens, amber browns, and russet reds of many handcrafted tiles, the new tiles dazzled the viewer with intricate patterns in jewel-bright hues. A high point of this design path was the Malibu Pottery, founded by May K. Ringe on her Malibu estate. Malibu Pottery produced stunning "Moorish" designs, vivid and complex, with abstract interlaced arabesques, butterflies, and peacocks, and even whole Persian rugs in ceramic, detailed down to the fringe.

Up north were several major potteries, including California Faience. It produced tile designed by architect Julia Morgan to outfit San Simeon, William Randolph Hearst's 1920s mansion, north of San Luis Obispo, California, in ceramic flowers, ships, and fantastical creatures.

The turn-of-the-century decades jostle with dozens of personality-rich potteries and tile makers, many short-lived. Some ventures were

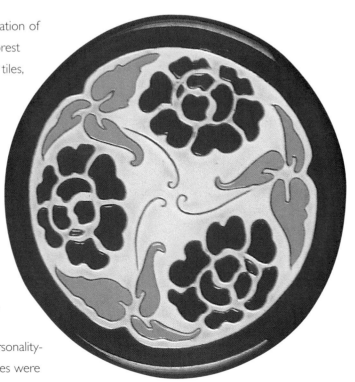

Above and right: Delicate flowers and a dreamy landscape were produced at Marblehead Pottery as part of artistic therapy for sanatorium patients.
Below: Immigrant girls learned a useful trade at Paul Revere Pottery in hand-painting soft-edged designs such as this pastel tree.

strictly dilettantish. Between 1877 and 1887, New York's "Tile Club," a group of artists, including painter Winslow Homer and architect Stanford White, met informally at each other's studios to paint tiles. Ceramics even served philanthropic purposes—historian Noel Riley cites the Marblehead Pottery, founded in 1905 as a therapeutic venture for "nervously worn-out" sanitarium patients, and the Paul Revere Pottery, a trade school for indigent immigrant girls.

ART AND BUSINESS

In contrast to America's handcrafted art tile workshops stood large, factory-based manufacturers. Zanesville, Ohio, was an early center of production. There, in 1876, the American Encaustic Tiling Company was founded and eventually grew into the largest tile company of its time, which extended into the 1930s. One of its employees was the German-born artist and sculptor Herman C. Mueller, who launched the Mueller Mosaic Tile Company in 1903, which became an industry stalwart. Mueller, a friend of

Left and below: Large tile factories, such as Ohio-based American Encaustic, were inspired by small craft-based potteries to produce their own art tiles, such as these allegorical representations of "Summer" and "Spring," finished in a delicate, translucent glaze.

Henry Chapman Mercer, based his firm in Trenton, New Jersey, which was another nexus for commercial tile companies. By the 1920s, California had become another high-volume production center, with Gladding, McBean Co., the largest West Coast tile concern.

The bread-and-butter seller for large commercial firms was unglazed geometric floor tile and other utility products. But most also found a profitable sideline in decorative *faience*—a factory-produced tile with a fashionably handmade look. "In the U.S., the large manufacturers were heavily influenced by the trends that evolved on the studio level," explains Taylor, of the Tile Heritage Society. "When they saw that the public loved handmade tiles, they would naturally use their technical expertise to get that effect." The actual amount of handwork varied with different products, but many

Right: Gladding, McBean & Co., the largest West Coast tile factory in the early twentieth century, produced such artfully decorative tile as these squares inspired by Mexican folk pieces. **Below:** The firm also met the demand for more intricate Moorish designs as displayed in this exterior border.

manufacturers, such as Mueller Mosaic, maintained studios to custom-craft special-order tiles.

This emphasis on the handcrafted look, Taylor points out, is one of the distinguishing characteristics of America's tile history, along with the predominance of matte glazes and relief designs. "The third characteristic is an abundance of designs that often reflect the American heritage or landscape," continues Taylor. "There are scenes, trees, animals, and people that we can instantly identify as our own."

As in England, prosperity fueled America's own turn-of-the-century industry, while maintaining the steady market for imported tile. Tile was the modern sanitary surface for kitchens, and for the increasingly common plumbed-in bathroom. Public buildings, business offices, train stations and subways, theaters and movie palaces, and that strictly American innovation, the lavish soda fountain, were all made splendid with tile. Tile historian Julian Barnard even tells of a frontier Fort Worth saloon's floor tiles that were inset with $20 gold pieces. It attracted such crowds of thirsty cowboys, thrilled to be walking over a fortune, that when pickax-wielding robbers stole the floor, the owner ordered a similar floor to be installed.

Such an anomaly aside, America's earlier art tiles tended to be classical, sometimes sentimental, with realistic, detailed designs. After the turn of the century, the designs became more stylized and rugged, or more exotically colorful, reflecting the exuberance of the Jazz Age.

TOWARD OUR TIMES

But such ebullience and a history of artistry were snuffed out by the Great Depression, which initiated some aesthetically lean decades for American tile. Only a few tile companies survived the 1930s, and after the U.S. entered World War II in 1941, they were largely diverted to supporting the war effort.

Ceramic tile shared in the post-war housing boom, but the tile produced were uniform, utilitarian squares, glazed in timid pastels. Commercial and public architecture favored a stripped-down International Style; homeowners were distracted by novel synthetic surfaces, such as linoleum, vinyl, terrazzo, and laminates.

But just as the Industrial Age carried the seeds of the Arts and Crafts movement, the reaction to utilitarian tile began in the 1960s and 1970s with a renewed interest in craft. "There were subtle hints that art was a factor — that tile could be beautiful," notes Taylor, "maybe with some variations in the glazes or decorative accents decaled or stenciled on." The late 1960s also saw the stirring of Postmodern architecture, which conceded that people desire ornament and individuality in their surroundings. By the 1980s, well-priced imports opened the range of design possibilities, often for clean-lined looks, with larger sizes, or quirkier, sometimes hand-painted products reflecting European traditions. And Americans were rediscovering their own vivid ceramic history: The Moravian Pottery in Doylestown, Pennsylvania; the Pewabic Pottery in Detroit, Michigan; and the Malibu Pottery's Adamson House are all open as working museums today.

A ceramic tile renaissance is now in full swing, as examined in Chapter 4 (beginning on page 53), with hundreds of tile artists, muralists, and mosaicists at work in small studios and factories. Just as in art tile's heyday, large manufacturers have noted this consumer interest and expanded their own offerings of distinctively decorative products. In showrooms, design magazines and books, in commercial settings, and in our own homes, the newest installment of tile's long history is now being written.

Above: A century ago, Moravian Pottery first produced such tiles as this, titled "Bee Hiving." Today, several historic firms are back in operation, joined by many new artistic tile makers.

CHAPTER 3

TODAY'S TILE

Manufactured Magic

Americans are more intrigued by ceramic tile than ever before. According to the U.S. Department of Commerce, our annual usage of ceramic tile has more than tripled over the last two decades. Beyond dry statistics, the more vivid testimony is the colorful smorgasbord of products available—a richness that can be a little overwhelming when it comes time for choosing. This chapter aims to be a guide or an overview of the categories of commercially produced tile, with some pointers on matching the product to the project. Within those categories, we will also hint at the range of design possibilities on the market.

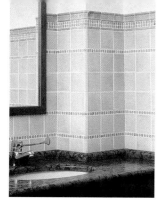

Above and below: Italian ceramic tile manufacturers now offer a wider range of subtle colors, trim pieces, and decorative motifs.

Previous pages: Accent tiles molded in high relief draw on a heritage of handmade tile.

Ours is an international marketplace. About two-thirds of America's tile is imported. Italy, the world's leading producer, contributes the largest share, followed by Spain and an international roster of exporters: Mexico, Brazil, and in lesser amounts France, England, and Germany, with several Asian countries making strong inroads. Such global competition has made the menu of commercially produced tiles wider, bolder, and more stylish.

But you can't choose tile by looks alone. The fundamental ceramic tile, a slab of fire-hardened clay, has been spun into a multitude of products, sometimes designated by confusing or loosely used terminology. The information in this chapter will help you to choose a tile for a particular job. But you should also discuss the particulars with a knowledgeable tile salesperson as well. Before the final decision, double-check the manufacturer's specifications, which rate the tile's physical properties according to industry standards.

If a tile passes the industry tests for dimensional standardization and durability, it is designated as standard grade. Tile that meets the technical requirements but has minor cosmetic defects is classified as second-grade or "seconds."

CERAMIC FAMILIES

Most broadly, ceramic tile divides between unglazed products, such as quarries, pavers, and terra-cottas, and glazed tiles, whether delicate decorative wall tiles or sturdier flooring. Mosaic is an industry term for a tile smaller than 2.4 inches by 2.4 inches, whether glazed or unglazed.

Unglazed tile is simply the fire-hardened clay slab, the same color throughout—either the natural clay color, from cream to buff to umber, or tinted with added minerals. Under different firing temperatures or kiln conditions, the same clay can produce different colors.

The common ground of many varieties of clay is fine-grained aluminum silicate, formed when certain rocks weather and decompose. But most clays used commercially include a variety of additives, mixed in by nature or more deliberately by skillful tile makers, which extend the clay, lend color, modify the firing temperature, add strength, or reduce shrinkage and cracking.

Commercially produced unglazed tiles are differentiated by the shaping method. For an extruded tile, moist, malleable clay is forced through a die; the emerging ribbon is sliced into squares or rectangles, generally with a crisp edge, a flat surface, and a grooved underside. Tiles produced by extrusion are often designated as quarry tiles. In dust-pressing, by contrast, the clay is partially dried, then ground, mixed, and rammed under high pressure into steel molds. Some are flat-backed; others have a grid or buttons pressed on the underside, which let air circulate around the tile in the kiln. Dust-pressed or molded products are often called pavers.

After shaping, the "green" tile is thoroughly dried because trapped moisture could warp or explode the clay body in the kiln. There, high heat removes the final traces of moisture and fuses the clay into a hard bisque. The firing temperature and duration determine the bisque's physical properties. Low-fired clay is porous, riddled with microscopic air-pockets where water and stains can intrude. A longer, hotter firing fills in those pores, as the minerals vitrify, or melt and fuse into a stronger, denser, less-absorbent matrix.

CATEGORIES OF TILE

In matching a tile to a particular purpose, the level of vitrification is the deciding factor. The American National Standards Institute (ANSI) spells out four categories of ascending vitrification and the corresponding water-absorption rates by weight:

◆ **Nonvitreous.** This tile has a water-absorption rate exceeding 7 percent. This unglazed, low-fired earthenware is prone to stains, and even when sealed is unsuitable for floors subject to wetness or heavy use. Properly treated, such tile may serve outdoors in dry, hot climates. In colder regions, the absorbed moisture, expanding with freezing temperatures, can crack and chip the tile.

◆ **Semivitreous.** The tile is produced in higher kiln temperatures for a 3- to 7-percent absorption rate. Such stoneware is suitable for most indoor floors, if properly sealed, and certain outdoor applications. Some products in this range are frost-proof.

◆ **Vitreous.** These products have an absorbency rating between 0.5 percent and 3 percent. High-fired stoneware can serve in most wet or high-traffic conditions and cold-climate exterior applications.

◆ **Impervious.** Fired at length at temperatures above 2,000 degrees Fahrenheit, these tiles have absorption rates below 0.5 percent, and are often referred to as porcelain. Such high-fired products are dense and stain resistant, require no sealing, and are durable and ready for wet or freezing conditions. But they carry a premium price tag, and the hard, nonabsorbent bodies are somewhat more difficult to cut and bond to the substrate during installation.

Above: Widely used in the early twentieth century, mosaic floors patterned in white-and-black one-inch "hexies" have a nostalgic aura. High-fired unglazed porcelain makes a durable, slip-resistant surface.

TILE TERMINOLOGY

To understand the differences between the various kinds of tile, their characteristics, and their likely applications, it is a good idea to become familiar with some basic definitions:

Quarry tiles. These tiles are tough, generally vitreous or semivitreous extruded flooring products. Commonly red, quarries can range into other earthy colors, often with natural variations and randomly flashed with dark streaks, caused by minerals reacting to the kiln's heat. Quarry tiles are at least ⅜ inch thick, in 3- to 12-inch squares, with some rectangles and hexagons available.

Pressed pavers. They may be precisely clean edged or deliberately rusticated with irregular outlines; some have a slightly pillowed profile with eased-down edges. In a high-use area, the rugged texture of pillowed squares may be tiring to stand on, and the recesses can trap dirt and wash water. A flat tile with a high, narrow grout line is easier to maintain.

Impervious porcelain pavers. First developed for commercial sites, they are increasingly popular for residential applications, commonly in 12-inch squares, though 4x6-inch "subway" rectangles or oversize 16- or 24-inch squares are also available. Small mosaic tiles, whether square, circular, or hexagonal, are often porcelain; this product category has seen something of a revival in today's "retro" kitchens and baths. Mosaics are factory-mounted in 12-foot-square sections with a mesh backing or attached to a paper face, which is dampened and peeled away after installation.

Terra-cotta. In Italian, "baked earth"—the term loosely designates thick-bodied, unglazed pavers, usually imported from the Mediterranean, Mexico, or South America. Their natural earthy hues are generally reddish brown but range into pink to ocher-yellow tones.

Terra-cotta varies in quality and price, depending on the country of origin and the manufacturing method. Some rustic terra-cottas, such as Mexican *saltillo* tiles (named for the original producing region) are hand-molded in wooden forms, complete with finger marks, wavy profiles, and irregular corners. Others are factory-made by extrusion or machine-molding, with either a rugged appearance or a sleeker look. For a price, you can even buy antique terra-cotta, reclaimed from European manors and villas.

Many terra-cottas are fired at low temperatures, creating a nonvitreous or semivitreous body. Even indoors, terra-cotta's absorbent surface generally requires careful periodic sealing and more

maintenance than other floor tiles. If you need something that is more heavy-duty, ask a knowledgeable tile salesperson to suggest a suitable product that captures a little of terra-cotta's timeless look.

Encaustic tile. A special category of unglazed ceramics is encaustic tile, with deep, imprinted designs filled in with contrasting clay—a medieval method reborn for the nineteenth-century Gothic Revival style. True encaustic tiles are pricey studio-made products, usually imported. Some durable matte-glazed, silk-screened tiles are now available that effectively mimic the classic patterns.

UNGLAZED, YET ARTFUL

Decoratively speaking, the solid, low-key appeal of unglazed tiles can be played up with geometry. Showier shapes, such as hexagons, octagons-and-squares, curvaceous ogee (or Moorish shapes), or any number of overall geometric patterns mixing sizes and shapes, can enliven an unglazed floor without losing its easygoing neutral quality. Brighter glazed inserts, bands of

Above: To jazz up the earthy tones of these unglazed tiles, the owners chose a classic hexagonal shape and added colorful glazed inserts. Unglazed quarry tiles generally need periodic sealing in a splash-prone kitchen environment.

contrasting mosaics, or clusters of patterned pieces break up the repetitive expanses of a large floor.

Porcelain pavers were first made in solid, matte colors or an understated speckled-granite look. Faux stone has proved perennially popular for floor tiles, both glazed and unglazed. But the effect has become a more sophisticated finish, realistically evoking coarser granite, travertine marble, limestone, and split slate. Textures can be highly polished and formal or present a warm aged appearance. Instead of repetitious patterns, new manufacturing technology allows for more random variations, and the combining of different-color clays for a more natural stone effect.

In a procedure that Spanish manufacturers call *rectificado*, computer-controlled water jets cut large-format tile with

Right: Rich glazed backsplash tiles contrast with the boldly geometric matte floor tile in a contemporary kitchen while adding warm, inviting color.

precisely calibrated edges, which can be laid with minimal grout joints to complete the illusion of a stone slab. The same high-tech cutting tools can "inlay" contrasting geometric inserts in a porcelain tile or create offbeat interlocking shapes.

Manufacturers of standard porcelain mosaic "pennies" or "hexies" offer a menu of attractive patterns, such as a Greek-key border or intricate latticework, delivered premounted for easy installation.

The porous surface of classic terra-cotta can be buffed with colored waxes, pickled with whitewash, or embellished with stenciled or hand-painted flourishes. Fragile raised or incised designs may be suitable only for walls.

A GLAZED LOOK

The word glaze derives from glass, and indeed the two are closely related. Early on, potters discovered that fusing a glassy layer to the ceramic surface rendered it more impermeable and more beautiful, catching the light and enriching the colors. The basic glaze recipe combines glass-forming minerals, such as silica and boron, with clays to add body, melting agents such as lead or soda, and metallic oxides providing a rainbow of colors.

Glazes also fuse art and science, as the ceramist juggles many variables to achieve the desired effect. The same oxide can produce radically different colors, depending on its reactions with the other glaze ingredients, the clay body underneath, and the kiln's temperature and atmosphere. Raw glaze ingredients may be fused into glass and ground into "frit," which often serves as the basis for somewhat more predictable commercially used glazes. Even modern manufacturing can't completely tame temperamental glazes, however, and different production runs may vary slightly in color.

Traditionally, the clay body was first fired to hardness, then glazed and returned to the kilns to produce a double-fired, or *bicottura* tile. Some highly

Below: Glasslike glazes give tile an impervious surface, and open up a realm of decorative flourishes, such as these pastel ivy leaves.

CATEGORIES OF TILE

Glazed tiles are rated for resistance to abrasion, and grouped according to their suitable applications, using a four-category Porcelain Enamel Institute (PEI) system:

◆ **Class I:** Walls only.

◆ **Class II:** Very light-use floors, such as a bath off a bedroom, where no footwear is the norm.

◆ **Class III:** Medium-use residential applications, such as family bath or kitchen.

◆ **Class IV:** Heavy-use residential applications, such as entries or kitchens with exterior entrances, or for commercial installations.

Newer guidelines now being drawn up by the International Standards Association (ISO) run a similar, but not exactly equivalent, ascending scale. The ISO scale extends to Class V, recognizing new super-durable, stain-resistant glazes, suitable for the most demanding commercial applications.

Though not required, some manufacturers also rate glazes with the Mohs hardness scale borrowed from geologists. It rates materials on a 1 to 10 scale, by the hardness of the material needed to scratch the surface—ranging from talc, at 1, to diamond, at 10. A Mohs rating of 5 or 6 translates into a medium-use tile, and 7 or 8 rating denotes a heavy-duty product.

decorated tiles may undergo a succession of progressively lower firings, as more delicate colors are added. More tiles today are single-fired or *monocottura* products, with glaze and raw-clay body fired together in one pass through the kilns. Cost-efficient single firing strongly bonds the glaze and tile but somewhat limits the decorative possibilities.

Glazed products divide between floor tiles, carefully rated and graded for wear and strength, and lighter, thinner, wall tiles. Countertop tiles also require sturdy glazes, plus resistance to the mild acids in certain foods and cleaners.

Porcelain pavers and thicker quarry tiles are sometimes finished with glaze. But most glazed floor tiles are single-fired, dust-pressed squares, often of red clays. Most are 12-inch squares, though larger formats, up to 24 inches, are also available.

Slip resistance is vital underfoot in a kitchen or entry subject to moisture and spills. Unglazed tiles, unless polished, tend to be fairly slip resistant, as is the pebbled texture of mosaics. In a commercial setting, where firm footing is an issue, designers will often specify a tile with a coefficient-of-friction rating of 0.6 or higher. Incised designs or grit added to glaze will increase the rating but also make the floor harder to clean.

GREAT WALLS

Durability is less an issue with wall tiles, so their glazes and textures run a wider range. Dust-pressed glazed wall tiles are often nonvitreous; inexpensive white gypsum-base bathroom squares are easily cut to fit around fixtures and lightweight and absorbent enough to grip the mortar quickly in a vertical installation. Yet because the glazed face is fairly impervious, such tiles, installed with water-resistant setting materials, frequently are installed in damp areas, such as a tub alcove.

Glazed wall tiles are most commonly 3-, 4 -, and 6-inch squares (though larger squares and rectangles are increasingly popular), and about ¼ to ⁵⁄₁₆ inch thick. Many have lugs

along the sides to ensure proper spacing. All tile sizes, like lumber dimensions, are nominal; the true dimensions may differ, as the manufacturer allows for a certain size of grout line. Some wall tiles are venturing into offbeat shapes, such as scallops and waves, triangles and hexagons, or free-form compositions of fruit, leaves, birds, and animals.

The glaze palette can run from saturated cobalt blue and scarlet red to whisper-soft pastels; they can present a face that is high-gloss, satiny, crackled, brushed, matte, or iridescent. Some wall tiles play with the unpredictable nature of glaze to produce colors richly varied, mottled, streaked, and pooled, which fashion a flowing whole when installed side by side. Textured surfaces and high-relief designs also play up the shifting colors. Taking the idea even further, multicolor field tiles subtly intermingle different glazes, such as pink and rust, with a golden undertone. Metallic looks, from soft pewter to dark steely tints and lush gold, add richness while remaining neutral in the color scheme.

Beyond the beautiful colors of the glaze itself is the realm of decorative tile, the industry term for anything with a picture or pattern added. In commercial production, most

Left: Because they needn't be particularly durable, wall tiles run a stylistic gamut. On this bathroom wainscot, the intense hue of the bricklike, glossy tiles is leavened by a sculpted, pale border and a bold molding.

Above: In a stove alcove, the dimensional profile of these decorative tiles and the satiny, variegated glaze evoke a handmade tile.

Below: Properly chosen trim tiles neatly cover an installation's raw edges. On this wainscot, the elaborate bull-nose moldings and a harlequin border edged between slim liner tiles add up to a tailored finish.

decorative motifs are silk-screened, though some are printed or stamped. Some manufacturers offer motifs on decals ready to be fired onto the tile of your choice with a protective glaze. Digitized printing technology can now reproduce pictures on tile with photographic precision —to put realistic pebbles or leaves across a bathroom floor, for instance.

Decorative tiles can be lined up into borders or scattered among plain field tiles. The classic motifs of flowers, foods, birds, and animals are abundantly available, both in traditional realistic interpretations or sleeker stylized versions. Tile designers also reach into a deep inventory of historical motifs: Art Nouveau abstracts, delft scenes, whimsical folk images, Victorian transfer prints, and vivid Moorish designs. You'll find truly antique images, as well, drawn from hieroglyphics, ancient runes, classical Roman or Greek images, cave art, fossils, and zodiac signs. A few mosaic manufacturers have even added a tiny embossed or silk-screened motif on each tile, to make a pattern within the pattern.

A special category of decorative tile includes the longer, narrower border tiles, also called liners, feature strips, or *listelli*, which can handsomely frame or break up a plain field. Dimensional moldings offer a particularly lush, architectural look, without necessarily adding a lot of color.

IN FULL TRIM

While decorative trim is designed to stand out, most commercially produced tile also offers functional trim that blends in and smoothes out the transitions around corners and between different materials. Practical trims include the following:

◆ **Bullnose.** A flat tile rounded over on one side, to make a smooth edge.

◆ **Cove tile.** A rounded, easier-to-clean inside corner where horizontal and vertical places meet, such as at the back of a counter.

◆ **Inside and outside corners.** Trim tiles that smooth out and protect these vulnerable points.

◆ **Quarter-round or bead.** A narrow, convex molding, used to trim sinks or cover the seam between tub and wall.

◆ **Bases or runners.** Trim tiles with rounded tops to fashion a baseboard above a tiled floor.

◆ **Stair-step tread.** A tile that juts out over the riser and often has slip-resistant texturing.

◆ **V-cap.** Trims for a counter's front, sometimes with a bumped-up edge to contain spills.

If you like a tile series that lacks functional trim, you have a few options. You may be able to special-order a field tile with a glazed edge, which might suffice to finish a final row. Unglazed tiles may be honed down to a smooth bullnose curve. During installation, tile edges can be mitered, to meet at a smooth right angle, although on an outside corner this sharp joint is more prone to breakage. Skilled installation can often compensate for lack of trim pieces, though such fine detail work increases the job costs. Finally, you may be able to use trim from another line—but beware of different thicknesses, which can complicate installation.

Above: At the outside corner, one-piece wraparound trim tiles protect a vulnerable edge. They frame the sink counter in a strong vertical band of bright blue, echoing the decorative floral tiles. Another special-purpose trim tile is used on the windowsill.

BUYING DECISIONS

Armed with basic information and a good understanding of the practical demands of your project, start shopping. Flooring stores and home centers offer basic products at good prices and quick in-stock delivery. But the broadest and most exciting selection is found in specialty tile showrooms. An architect or designer can give you access to to-the-trade showrooms with even more exotic offerings. This is not the time for one-stop shopping. Visiting different showrooms widens the range of possibilities and provides valuable ideas. Showroom vignettes and catalog pictures give you a clearer idea of how a tile looks en masse, which may differ from the impression made by an isolated sample.

Discuss your project with a knowledgeable salesperson, who can suggest suitable products and bring out additional catalogs and sample boxes to expand the choices. Given the limits of color printing, it's risky to place a final order from a catalog picture without seeing actual samples. Once you've narrowed the field, borrow or buy samples to examine them in the intended

Below: When combining solid-color tile into an eye-catching patchwork, the design should be carefully worked out on paper for the proper visual balance. You can double-check the exact amount of each color; order a few extras for possible breakage during installation.

room by artificial and natural light and to test against the other furnishings. If you own the sample, run your own tests on it—scuff it with a shoe, scrape it with a pipe, drip some oil on it, and see how it cleans up.

Specifications. Before you purchase the product, check its specifications in the manufacturer's literature. Ascertain the tile's actual (rather than nominal) dimensions, and provide careful measurements of the intended room so that the salesperson can accurately estimate the tile and trim needed. Generally 5 to 10 percent extra is allowed for breakage, cutting, and replacing broken tiles in years to come. If you're working with an installer, he or she should order the tile and take responsibility for the quantities. Ask whether unopened cases may be returned. Because custom or special orders are usually not returnable, you may ask the retailer to double-check the amount ordered.

Delivery. How long will it take to receive the tile? Products stocked locally may be delivered within the week, but for a special order you may have to plan around a lead time of four to eight weeks or even longer to avoid a scheduling glitch. When the tile arrives on-site, check that the boxes are from the same shade lot, and visually examine several tiles from each carton for consistent colors. Questions of tile quality should be discussed with the retailer before installation.

Cost. Tile prices run the gamut, though efficient manufacturing and distribution have long held down the cost of basic products. Solid-color, white glazed bathroom wall squares are the most economical. Floor tiles are higher and can get quite expensive for high-fired porcelains. Both are priced per square foot (psf). Special decorative tiles are often priced per piece, and trims by the running foot. Factor in the cost of installation, which varies by region, the complexity of the job, and the experience of the installer.

If budget is a consideration, keep an eye out for dealers' closeouts of tiles that have been discontinued, overstocked, or left over from a large project. Less-expensive seconds with slight cosmetic problems may go unnoticed mixed into the less-obtrusive areas of a field of unblemished tiles. But be wary of trying to economize too far. Tile is a long-lasting purchase, and a few hundred dollars spent at the outset is amortized over a long product life. Installation is also a fixed part of the total: it costs just as much to install cheap tile.

If the budget is less of an issue, and even the far-flung offerings on today's market aren't yielding up the tile of your dreams, consider having tile made to order—as discussed in the next chapter.

Above: Tile is versatile enough to cover multiple surfaces, such as the floors and tub walls in this master bath. Before the final purchase, check the manufacturers' specifications to make sure the product is rated for its intended use.

CHAPTER 4

ONE-OF-A-KIND TILE

A Craft Reborn

Ceramic tile began as the work of human hands, creating something enduring and extraordinary from the most common of materials. In the nineteenth century, as mechanization was making tile an everyday commodity, the Arts and Crafts movement looked back to celebrate the honest efforts and creative vision of the individual artisan. And in our own era of high-tech mass-production, we're seeing a similar resurgence of the handmade or hand-painted tile in all its vibrant individuality.

Right: Art tiles can offer uncommon designs such as this turtle by Joan Gardiner, escaping its painted frame. **Below:** Or they can heark back to more classical motifs, such these custom-painted old-world birds and flowers. **Previous page:** A tonally varied backsplash is an experiment in color.

"More craftspeople and artists are working with the tile medium today than ever before," says Joseph Taylor, president of the Tile Heritage Society. "It's not just a utilitarian surface," he continues, "but a means of bringing color and texture and design into the home."

Handmade Trend. Big manufacturers, too, are feeling the phenomenon's influence. Their trade organization, the Tile Council of America (TCA), has added a membership category for studio tile makers. "Handmade and custom-made products are definitely a trend," concurs Bob Daniels, TCA's executive director. "It's not a big market in square footage, but it generates excitement—homeowners love the idea of a mural on the backsplash or scattering some hand-decorated inserts on a standard tile floor." A growing number of retailers, he points out, include some special "art tile" lines alongside their regular offerings. Moreover, the last 20 years has seen the blossoming of specialty tile showrooms, representing handmade products from a variety of domestic and international sources.

Some of those special tiles are imported from countries with long traditions in handmade tiles. Certain delftware patterns have been in the repertoire of Royal Makkum in the Netherlands for centuries. From Mexico come lively *talavera* tiles with freely sketched flowers and birds; from Portugal, *culinarios* of

vegetables and hanging game. Traditional Italian craftspeople still create folk patterns and painterly Renaissance motifs in vivid tints. The products of these European workshops are widely available through the higher-end retailers, sometimes with customizing options as well.

Domestic sources range from small one- and two-person studios, to flourishing potteries employing dozens of artisans. Some lovingly reproduce or reinterpret historic tile motifs, while others concentrate on original designs. Several of America's well-known nineteenth-century art potteries are serving as living museums of the craft, using the original molds, shaping methods and glaze formulas.

A LOOK AT THE LINEUP

Highly individual by its nature, handmade tile spans a diversity of methods and styles. Some tile artists take a painterly approach, concentrating on the surface—they use a manufactured bisque, the fired-clay body, as the canvas for hand-painted design. Effective hand-painting demands precision and an understanding of the palette of glazes, particularly for custom work. Less-expensive tiles may involve some silk-screening or printing, albeit in custom colors.

For many small studios, painting in glaze on a manufactured tile is more logistically feasible: It sidesteps the labor- and equipment-intensive production process to focus on the fine brushwork. Field tiles to accompany the scattered artworks or a central mural are readily available and modestly priced. Clean-edged, machine-made tiles, installed with minimal grout lines, let the design flow smoothly from tile to tile. They effectively evoke the popular dust-pressed wares with intricate, lithographed transfer patterns in the Victorian era.

Below: Crisp machine-made tiles can be laid with minimal grout joints, making a smooth, continuous surface for hand-painted murals, such as this custom portrait of a home, complete with a portrait of the family pet.

Glaze Tradition.

Hand-painting in glaze has a long lineage. Makers of majolica and delft tiles prized the white tin glaze because it held fast to

intricately painted designs, often in large-scale, polychrome murals. Such loose, spontaneous florals and narrative scenes, in an old-world style, are still reproduced by American tile artists. But the decorative ideas can swing from precisely drawn dragonflies and ladybugs to splashing dolphins to cartoonishly bright geometrics. If you're inclined toward history, you can find artistic interpretation of Roman columns, Amish quilt patterns, sponged or stenciled country motifs, impressionistic landscapes, or "aesthetic" peacocks and sunflowers.

California-based Designs in Tile offers hand-painted custom designs and reproduction patterns, ranging from intricate nineteenth-century Morris and De Morgan designs to folkier delft and Pennsylvania Dutch motifs. They are applied to the firm's own tiles or on a variety of commercially available bisques, suited to different installations. Several manufacturers maintain a studio division to custom-paint murals to suit a customer's whim, whether it's for a portrait of the family home for the entry wall, or the family's Airedales for the backsplash in the kitchen.

Left: Hand-painted tile murals give a custom look to an all-white kitchen. **Above:** Adding dimension to the art tile, Ellie Stein molded a panel in high-relief. **Below:** Intricate, overlapped leaves by Michelle Griffoul also have a tactile appeal.

THE RIGHT MIX FOR TILE

Many tile artists begin with the fundamental clay. Here they match wits with a temperamental material, exploring many possible formulations, offering different textures, working qualities, firing temperatures, and decorative possibilities. A clay must be smooth and "plastic" enough to work but not too fine-grained, or it may shrink and crack as it dries. Such clay is opened up by adding coarse, non-plastic material such as fine sand or "grog," a ground-fired clay—but too coarse a mixture will not fuse properly. Fluxing agents help the clay melt and fuse, but such additives in excess will cause deformation or "bloating" from trapped gas. Clay "remembers" stresses put on it during shaping, and a piece may leave the kiln revealing an unexpected twist.

Despite such intricacies, or perhaps because of them, tile makers can get poetic about clay: many admit to "falling in love with clay," at the first hands-on meeting. In the preface to a no-nonsense textbook of clay and glaze formulations, author and potter James Chappell concedes that "Forming clay, creating something that has form and beauty, is a fever in the blood."

Liquefied clay slip can be poured into permeable plaster molds to produce finely detailed, high-relief patterns. But potters are more drawn to working hands-on with malleable

clay. To form tiles, the material can be hand-pressed into wooden or plaster molds or rolled and cut like sugar cookies. Hand-carved blocks can stamp the soft surface into a high-relief or incised design; lace, burlap, coins, or leaves might imprint a gentler texture. When the clay slab has dried "leather hard," the artist can carve the surface, apply small bits of clay, build up subtle designs with brushed-on slip, or tube-line a raised pattern to fill with pools of glaze.

Clay Carpentry. Florida tile artist Peter King specializes in large-scale ceramic frameworks for fireplaces, doorways, or windows, as well as freestanding sculptures. He begins his "clay carpentry" with large sheets of clay, layered and sculpted on the studio floor. The finished piece is then glazed, sliced into pieces, and numbered for re-assembly after the firing. King recalls his inspiration at first seeing the tilework installed at the nineteenth-century Moravian Pottery. "I was always working to make my tiles flatter and squarer, and these were anything but," he recalls, "Instead it was this undulating surface that caught the light, with each tile different, but the whole having this very powerful, organic feeling."

Above: Tile artist Peter King creates grand architectural ceramics such as a hearth evoking a chambered nautilus. **Right:** Framed in colorful mosaics and a twining border, Karen Koblitz fashioned a display shelf covered in sculptural tiles.

And while the tile must be well made to be a practical architectural finish, artists and homeowners gravitate to handmade tile for that spirit of irregularity and individuality. Much of today's handmade tile pays homage to the Arts and Crafts era, with molded high- or low-relief designs, for a bold, sculptural quality that dramatically sets it apart from most mass-produced tile. Designs may be intricate abstracts, or derive from natural references—flowers, trees, landscapes, birds, fish, and animals—often with strong, stylized outlines. Another rich inspiration is early twentieth-century California tilework, both the mellow, naturalistic Batchelder designs and the lush, colorful "Moorish" patterns of Malibu Tile, now reproduced by several art tile makers.

Many artists have also adopted traditional decorative motifs from sources far beyond tile-work, such as bold, African-inspired animals crafted in rugged matte textures and earthy hues by artist Frank Giorgini, in Freehold, New York. Kilim rugs, Celtic runes, Grecian mosaics, Provençal fabrics, or images of jackrabbits and barbed wire from the Old West—all have been reinterpreted for ceramics by today's artists. Computers can reproduce digitized photographic images with startling accuracy on the tile surface with heat-sensitive inks, which are then glazed for durability.

Below: In lush, variegated glazes, Motawi Tile offers a floral tile in glowing Art Nouveau hues, and gives a fireplace the matte surfaces and sculptural designs of the Arts and Crafts era.

GLAZE—CREATIVE CHEMISTRY

What distinguishes many handcrafted tiles from their commercial cousins is the quality of the glaze. Hand-applied, sometimes multilayered glazes can exhibit rich variations as they spread across the slightly irregular hand-finished surface, and take on a deep inner glow, whether glossy, "dead-matte," satiny, waxy, or iridescent. The blend of glass-making minerals, clays, and metallic oxides are dull when applied, but react in the kiln's intense heat to blossom into color.

Even more than the clay itself, glaze is intriguing in its complexities, with radically different effects achieved with a slight shift in the glaze recipe, a variation in the kiln temperature or atmosphere, or the choice of underlying clay. There's a certain suspense until the piece comes out of the kilns. Even an errant fingerprint on the bisque can fault a finish. "Glaze is a beautiful thing to work with—I like its high jinks," says Karim Motawi, half of the sister-and-brother team behind Michigan's Motawi Tileworks, a source of bold geometric tiles and sculptural Arts and Crafts–style patterns. "It can be controlled," she continues, "only to a certain point."

Left: Hand-applied raku glazes are randomly transformed in the firing into a mottled, crazed, and varied finish, such as plays across these iridescent tiles by Penny Truitt.

Right: This unique mosaic backsplash was created with tiles broken and reassembled in a free-form flow.

Far right: Mosaics can also be as precisely pictorial as these dolphins playing in the waves in a pool-house shower.

On a relief pattern, a specially formulated glaze might melt off the high spots or pool in the recesses, shading a green into brown, or blue into olive, or a brown into a pink at the edges.

Many of these hand-applied glazes derive from closely guarded recipes of Arts and Crafts–era ceramists. The nineteenth-century founder of Fulper Pottery hid a sheaf of formulations in the family attic, where his granddaughters later discovered them and put back into production many of the lush finishes, such as a "leopard-skin" glaze mottled with natural hues.

While some glazes achieve their effects with precise chemical formulation, others depend on randomness. In *raku* ceramics (from a Japanese phrase translated as "happiness through chance" or "enjoyment of freedom"), the molten piece is pulled from the kiln and drenched in water, giving the glaze crackled, iridescent variations. Sometimes the glowing ceramic is first dropped on inflammable straw or sawdust, which ignites to add dark, carbonized streaks.

MOSAIC BITS AND PIECES

Another flourishing segment of the custom-tile market is the handmade mosaic, which breaks free of tile's orderly, expected grid. Even the most standard porcelain mosaics from large manufacturers can be special-ordered in custom patterns, such as an intricate Grecian border, a central medallion, or a monogram, factory-mounted on mesh, ready for installing.

In the hands of mosaic artists, tiny preformed tiles, or *tessarae,* come together in even more imaginative and free-flowing images that wrap abstract or pictorial images around curves and corners. Some are strikingly realistic, creating pictures carefully shaded and toned from piece to piece, sometimes hearkening to classical pavements of Greece and Rome. Others are crisp, graphic, and contemporary.

Most high-spirited of all are custom-created *pique-assiette,* or "broken-dish," mosaics that bring together random, broken pieces of tile or china—or even shells, stones, or glass—into a tactile, one-of-a-kind finish. Some mosaic artists even make their own custom-glazed tiles, only to break them into bits. Working on-site, the artist may set the pieces into a thick bed of mortar and carefully bring them to level; the mortar becomes an integral part of the pattern. Or the artist may work in the studio, assembling the pieces on mesh for thinset installation.

Intensive, on-site handwork makes one-of-a-kind mosaics expensive. As an alternative, several firms produce pre-mounted murals, sized to be dropped into a field of standard tiles as a distinctive centerpiece.

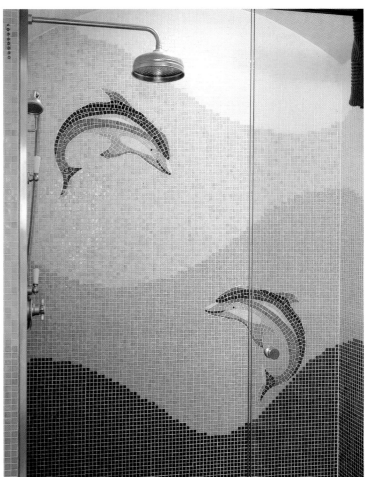

WORKING METHODS

How does a homeowner choose and work with a showroom, studio, or individual artist on a one-of-a-kind tile project? A useful first step is exploring the possibilities in books, magazines, Web sites, and showrooms. Try to clarify what you seek, without closing the door to the creative expertise you'll be paying for. "An artist doesn't particularly want a client to hand over a picture and say 'Make this,' " says ceramist Peter King. "But if someone can say, 'I want a Mediterranean feeling, and I like large-scale patterns,' or 'The house is filled with Victorian antiques,' that's somewhere to begin."

If you're working with an interior designer or architect, he or she may provide leads on local

CUSTOM-TAILORED TILE

Selecting a handcrafted tile begins with deciding on the effect you're after —exotic, classical, dignified, whimsical. Sometimes art tiles are applied lavishly, in great expanses. But they are also effectively used in small doses as a panel, border, or as scattered decoration in a more understated field.

Above: Artist Ellie Stein's jungle mural runs from tile to tile in bold colors and forms.

Above: A hand-painted bouquet has a quiet charm. **Left:** This hand-painted animal border on a bath backsplash reflects Colorado wildlife.

craftspeople and access to highly specialized tile showrooms, rife with handmade offerings.

Industry references, such as the Tile Heritage Society's Resource Directory, can provide leads to some local artists, as may the art department of a nearby university. For custom work, there's an advantage to working with someone local, to facilitate the give-and-take of the process.

Large, well-established potteries, and many smaller firms publish catalogs of popular offerings. Most also keep a portfolio of finished projects. Examine these with an eye toward finding an artist who's a good fit with your intended project. "Someone who's great at molding high-relief wildflowers might not be the person you'd ask to hand-paint a nude," says ceramist Karim Motawi "You'll get better results if you play to an artist's proven strengths, rather than ask them to work with unfamiliar techniques or materials."

Once the field is narrowed, you might meet for a free initial consultation, where you can look through the catalogs, portfolios, and samples; discuss the scope of your project; and toss around some ballpark cost estimates. As with any designer, take along color chips, fabrics, pictures, or objects that help convey your vision.

"Customers are buying something they can't see, so we do all we can to help them visualize," says Genevieve Sylvia, a design director at Pewabic Pottery. "We show them lots of previous projects and enough samples so they can see the glaze's variations—they have to love the whole range."

Top: The Restoration Center deftly reproduces early Batchelder tile designs.
Above: Leo Peck's sculptural floral fountain also hints at historical precedents.

A Practical Art

Most handmade tiles are meant for interior walls, though some are high-fired in the stoneware range, with frost-proof bodies and durable glazes for floors and exteriors. The tile artist should be able to guide you concerning the appropriate uses.

Business practices vary among firms. Custom design work may be estimated up front, then billed at an hourly rate or at a set price up to a certain number of proposed sketches.

Because a discretionary project may not be done right away, separating the costs for the design from the actual production of tile keeps the money advanced and the work done in reasonable sync.

If a tile has been chosen from the studio's catalog or portfolio, perhaps with small modifications, there's less up-front design work. The project may then be lumped into one price, usually with half due as a down payment and the remainder at delivery. A final design may be drawn to scale for the specific location, to serve as a map for the installer. Extra tiles are usually produced, because replacements might be hard to create with exactness later.

"With handmade tile you need an installer who appreciates the irregularities," notes Pewabic's Sylvia, "and who has

Above: Handmade tiles demand skilled installation to accommodate any irregularity. **Below:** A free-form work like Michelle Griffoul's cornucopia needs artful placement.

an aesthetic sense about laying out the tiles with a pleasing dispersion of the varied colors." By experimenting in a "dry run," before affixing the tiles, an installer can gracefully balance the tonal variations. A few tile studios install their own products, but most will recommend some specific tried-and-true installers. A staffer may also be on hand to supervise the work.

A wider grout line may be necessary to accommodate the tile's irregularities and aesthetically to complete an old-fashioned look. For wide joints, sand is often added to strengthen the grout. Sanded grouts must be handled with care, as they might scratch a delicate glaze.

Grout. The grout's color plays into the final effect, particularly in tilework that flows with varied tints. Highly contrasting grouts, whether light or dark, tend to stand out. Conversely, a grout matched to the tile's background pushes the decorative motifs to the foreground. With the deep, lustrous Craftsman-style glazes, a dark-to-medium gray or chocolate-brown grout is fairly neutral and recedes from view to frame each square.

Above: Renée Habert Stonebraker and James Stonebraker designed this two-part framed tile as a limited-edition wall piece.

COST CONCERNS

Handcrafted ceramics are an expensive medium for the artist, entailing an uneven flow of work, considerable overhead, frequent experimentation, and somewhat unpredictable materials. So handmade tile carries a hefty price tag, widely varying with the materials and the techniques, along with potentially higher installation costs. Field tiles are usually priced per square foot. Decorative pieces are priced per tile and the borders by the running foot.

To control costs, you may use handcrafted tile sparingly. While a custom-crafted backsplash could cost thousands of dollars, a length of sculpted border might add great panache for a fraction of the cost. Custom tile makers can often suggest commercial tiles that would be compatible go-withs, such as an oversize quarry tile to offset small, stylized Arts and Crafts–style rosettes. Because tile is a natural material, decorative pieces can harmonize as inserts to wood, marble, stone, or slate.

Ask whether the studio sells off acceptable seconds or perfectly fine overruns left from another job at reduced prices. There might be just enough to cover a small project or to add a stunning accent.

Even with costs trimmed back, handmade tile is a luxury. Yet, to put it into perspective, consider that what you're buying and integrating into your home, as Taylor of the Tile Heritage Society observes, is not just tile, "but a piece of art that becomes part of everyday life."

Above: In a bit of ceramic artistry, this broken-tile mosaic border above a cooktop accents a field of simpler squares.

CHAPTER 5

DESIGNING WITH TILE

Imagine the Possibilities

Ceramic tile is a unique finishing material but is still subject to the usual decorating concerns—issues of harmony and variety, scale and proportion, color and texture. Though the planning starts with the big picture, of practical needs and the desired overall impression, those general goals must be worked out in very particular choices. Which design elements will star in the space and which will be solid supporting players? As you make these aesthetic decisions, you can decide how ceramic tile might advance the room's overall plan. Clearly stating the tile's role in the decoration also helps narrow the large field of products when the time comes to shop.

LAYING THE GROUNDWORK

Professional designers first approach a project on a practical level, analyzing the space and its intended uses in some detail to arrive at a "program." Will the room be family oriented: bright and cheery and prepared for hard knocks? Or will it be an elegant showplace reserved for sedate entertaining? Maybe it's an efficient home office ready for client visits, a festive dining room, or a sun room facing tracked-in dirt and dripping potted plants.

PHYSICAL REALITIES

Think about the room's dimensions and how they drive the plans. Tight quarters may inspire you to use every space-enhancing trick, or you may choose to emphasize the coziness. An awkward, broken-up space might gain from the restful unity of a simple tile grid, while a bland box calls out for rich borders and trims. In an open floor plan, neighboring rooms enter into consideration. Tile effectively links spaces together or makes a graceful demarcation between functional areas. The same tough floor tile might be shared between the kitchen and family room, but run on the square in one room and then shifted to the diagonal in the next. Or a fancy backsplash tile could reappear on the family room fireplace as an echoing detail.

Previous pages: For a casual garden room, brick-like pavers exude the properly rugged simplicity.
Below: Sleek white floor tiles with black diamond insets complement the easy formality in a dining room with Queen Anne overtones.

A ROOM'S AMBIANCE

A history-rich reproduction tile pattern evokes a convincing period or regional flavor, either in a painstakingly restored historic home or an ordinary tract house. But most homeowners seek to capture an era's spirit or a certain level of formality rather than strict historical accuracy. A sleek modern tile might jar with a rustic Colonial den, yet suit a polished Queen Anne dining room harking back to the same era.

Deciding on the room's intended ambiance provides

a useful organizing principle for your design, particularly if you enjoy an eclectic mix of furnishings and finishes. Should the final effect be formal or informal, prim or rugged, challenging or cozy-comfortable? To give substance to such abstract ideas, try keeping a file of clippings, sample chips, advertisements, or brochures showing rooms and products that seem to capture what you're after. Then look for connections: Are the forms bold and hard-edged or fluid? Do the rooms bustle with clutter and color, or are they serenely stark? Do certain colors recur? As an added bonus, a picture can help you communicate to a designer or salesperson exactly what you envision as "homey" or "sophisticated."

FOCAL POINTS

But just because a room should, in Edith Wharton's phrase "speak with one voice," a satisfying interior need not be all the same. It needs high points that command atte-tion—a painting, a window, a dramatic pattern, a fireplace—supported by quieter elements. Design ideas, and the requisite shopping, usually start with the strongest, most-limiting factors: it's easier to track down plain solid-color tiles to go under an antique rug than vice versa.

Which role will tile play in your design? More often tile serves as an attractive low-key

Above: To make a collection of majolica the focal point of their living room, the owners chose a fireplace of soft, neutral-colored square tiles.

Above: A bay window is a natural focal point in any room, but the framework of decorative tile in blue-and-white has a fresh folk-art feeling that puts it at center stage in a country kitchen.

background. Homeowners who enjoy change and novelty in their surroundings or are concerned that the house have broad appeal at resale may prefer their tile handsome but understated. Such an approach reserves brighter colors and robust patterns for more easily changed components like wallcoverings, paint, and furniture.

But tile easily steps into a starring role. A bold, perhaps custom-made tile or an unusual pattern or color combination, even of standard products, fashions a natural focal point. Even a small quantity of dramatic tile is eye-catching and should be placed for maximum impact—centered in the tub wall, on the backsplash, along the chair rail, opposite a mirror, or circling a fireplace.

A POWERFUL PALETTE

We respond emotionally to color—hard and bright, soft and misty, earthy and mellow—as it instantly sets a room's mood. Designers often think of the spectrum of choices arranged in a wheel, with one color shading into the next between the pigment primaries of red, yellow, and blue equidistant on the wheel. One side represents warm hues in the red and yellow family, which tend to be upbeat and energizing in their stronger forms. The cooler greens and blues of the other half suggest a refreshing serenity. But colors go far beyond their "warm" versus "cool" stereotypes—a turquoise blue can electrify a room, while a soft rose is calming.

Below: The tile colors you choose immediately convey the room's mood. In an eat-in kitchen, the appetizing golds and tans in the mottled field tiles and the charming border convey a cordial sense of hospitality.

Above: Colors opposite each other on the color wheel tend to enhance each other. In this turn-of-the-century house, tile extends across wainscots and moldings in a complementary pairing of pink and green, suitably toned down for the classic Art Nouveau designs.

COLOR SCHEMES

Most of us can name a favorite color or two, and many well-loved interiors start just there. A favorite hue can launch a variety of color schemes:

◆ **Monochromatic** rooms spin the color into its lighter tints and darker shades, often relieved with some neutrals.

◆ **Analogous** schemes link a chosen color with a neighboring, related hue on the color wheel, such as a yellow-green paired with yellow. These schemes tend to have a harmonious and restful effect.

◆ **Complementary** plans pair a color with its complement (the color opposite it on the wheel, such as an orange with blue or yellow with violet, for a lively contrast that enriches both colors.

If such opposing schemes sound a bit garish, remember that each color represents a range of intensities. The blue-orange duo might translate into an earthy terra-cotta with turquoise inserts, or a soft peach wall tile with pencil-thin navy trim. In complementary pairings, one color should predominate, while the other provides the sharpening accent. Generally, the more powerful and bright a color is, the less of it is needed to make a statement.

Contrasts change our color perceptions. Black makes accompanying colors seem deeper and more vivid, as demonstrated by Moorish *cuerda seca* patterns, with their bold black outlines. With white, hues appear lighter and brighter, as in ebullient Italian majolica, with bright brush-stroked pictures on creamy white.

Other color interactions are less predictable. Warm colors tend to make their companion hues seem cooler, and vice versa. For instance, the same shade of red seems warmer and more orange in contrast with cool blue and takes on a cooler, more purple tinge alongside a strong yellow. Color combinations follow no strict rules. Unusual juxtapositions can be refreshing and create a one-of-a-kind look with ordinary products. But because tile is so long lasting, it's even more important to live with the samples a few days and determine that the proposed combination wears well.

A Quest for Color
Early on, tile makers found bright red to be the most elusive color. Glazes in shades of blue from copper and cobalt were more reliable and the most widely used.

Left: A backsplash of warm peach tiles, accented with a bright, cool checkerboard of blue and white is an example of attractive opposites.

Color can visually reshape a space: a tiny bathroom seems larger tiled in light, cool tints, which seem to recede from view. Warm, bold colors appear to advance, and might, for instance, draw in the far wall of an overly long room. Similar colors, perhaps with floors and walls in different sizes of the same tile, blend in irregularities and promote a spacious feeling, while strong contrasts are dramatic and give definition to a plain, boxy room. In a long, narrow space, an "area rug" of decorative tile minimizes the bowling-alley effect.

Color Choices. Ceramic finishes give color a special character. The unglazed surface, either in natural clay colors or tinted, has an earthy, solid quality, while a glaze heightens colors with a light-catching shimmer. Color choices in tile also carry historical connotations. Potters long ago achieved a vivid, reliable blue with cobalt, so blue and white is a classic ceramic pairing, from intricate Islamic tilework to the sweetness of country delftware. Art Nouveau is suggested in flowery purples and pinks and leafy blue-greens, while urbane Art Deco is more streamlined to neutrals and metallics. Earthy browns, reds, and turquoise can play into Southwestern or Mediterranean schemes, while energetic pastels could set the tone for a high-spirited retro-Fifties room.

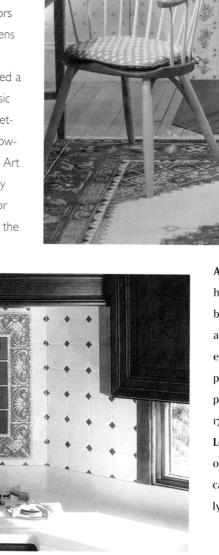

Above: Because of its long history in tile making, a blue-and-white pairing is an evocative color choice, especially in dainty Delft patterns recalling those produced by the Dutch in the 17th century.

Left: Tilework in bold blocks of intense blue on white can be a dramatic and equally effective treatment.

CLASSIC MIXERS

The U.S. tile market is dominated by neutral colors: white or off-white is the color most often sold. A classic choice, white goes with everything, reflects light, and brightens its companions. Manufacturers have diversified this salable category, so you can find white that's hard-edged and high tech or pearly and romantic, perhaps softened by outlines with a handmade look.

In each characterization, white is fresh and clean; however, without some enlivening accessories, it risks seeming clinical. Bathrooms in the 1920s and 1930s reveled in that modern, hygienic look, as seen in today's nostalgic rooms of white brick-shaped "subway" wall tiles and porcelain mosaic floors. White softened to a creamy tint maintains many of its advantages, to gentler effect.

Black, though neutral, is strong and dramatic, and often reserved for accents. Shades of gray tend to be more versatile and sophisticated. Grays used in decorating often carry a tinge of blue, taking it toward a stone color, or a warmer hint of pink or sand. Still, gray tilework

Below: Perennially popular white tile enhances the light and the feeling of space. An interesting play of texture and pattern, such as these "subway" bricks, gives the room a nostalgic and distinctive personality.

may need the help of lively accents to avoid dreariness.

All tints and shades of brown seem right for earthy tile. Even in glazed tiles, the natural hues from pale sand to umber are warm, congenial, and easy to keep. Deep russet quarries and terra-cottas can underpin a rustic room or warm up a modern space. Bright, glazed insets team up charmingly with unglazed squares.

Color Effects. Neutrals sometimes carry a hint of another hue, which must be considered in the color scheme. For example, red accessories may contrast crisply with tile-work in a cool, pale sand, yet seem a bit overwarm if the sandy tint has a pinkish cast. To discern these underlying hues, hold the ambiguous tile against paint chips in very definite colors and see which hue it pick ups.

If you lean toward low-key colors, don't overlook how tone, texture, and pattern create exciting effects without losing the desired neutrality. Even a plain white wall can be revved up with a play of shapes, maybe running successive rows of triangles, squares, and rectangles. Incised or molded patterns, such as a rope molding in deep relief, or an interplay of matte and glossy glazes provides visual and tactile pleasure.

Though technically a mixable neutral, a faux-stone

Above: White-tiled counters and backsplashes with details of black and gray are neutral but graphically striking in a modern kitchen.

Left: White can lean toward the warm or cool side. This creamy tiled wainscot blends with the straw hue of the upper walls for a cozy effect, enhanced by a classic turned-rope trim.

ceramic-tile floor presents a rich, complex surface. With new technology that creates more natural-looking random patterns, tile can effectively mimic limestone, slate, coarse travertine, elegant marble, or even a spread of pebbles with a mosaic-like appeal. Touches of metallic glazes in sophisticated shades of copper, pewter and gunmetal, or luxurious gold and silver

remain fairly neutral in a color scheme, yet have a lush, light-catching character.

Lighting strongly influences the color choices. We perceive color when pigments selectively absorb some wavelengths of light and reflect others back to our eyes. Because different kinds of light have characteristic collections of wavelengths, they can dramatically affect our color perceptions—a sample can undergo a sea change between the showroom and the home.

With increasingly energy-efficient windows, today's architecture emphasizes natural light and opening up rooms to the outdoors. Rooms facing west and

Above: With new manufacturing technology, ceramic tiles can more realistically mimic the textures of natural stone. Faux stone has a strong presence, yet mixes easily with other hues and textures.

south garner more natural light. A room with a cool northern exposure might benefit from a lighter, warmer palette of finishes. Or you might use refreshing blues and greens to cool off a room that bakes in the afternoon sun. Mexican or Middle Eastern ceramics typically play a cooling white background against vivid motifs in colors that stand up to the intense sunlight.

Artificial Light. In modern life we nevertheless tend to see our homes more often by artificial light. Standard fluorescents play up cooler blues and greens, though "deluxe warm white" bulbs are more balanced. Incandescent lights seem "warmer" because they enhance the yellow and red portion of the spectrum, while halogen bulbs are brighter and whiter.

Try to examine the tile samples in the room where they'll be installed, or at least under the same type of lighting. View tiles as they'll be used: hold wall tiles vertically, and lay floor tiles underfoot; move them to different areas of the room. The same tile might seem slightly darker on the walls, since the lighting, usually from overhead sources, may not be so direct.

Above: The strong line of horizontal tile border, such as this foliate design, draws the eye across the room in a calm, space-enhancing flow.

PATTERN PLAYS

You can't use tile without thinking about pattern on two different levels: the variations on the basic overall grid and the designs that might embellish individual decorative tiles.

Shapes are part of the exciting news in tile design today, as manufacturers and artisans are creating interlocking patterns with curves, waves, and scallops, or stylized leaves and birds.

Geometry enlivens even simple neutral tiles. By adding in more than one color, a custom look can be created with standard products., The patchwork becomes truly striking. Any "random" effect should be carefully worked out on graph paper or a computer. Some homeowners even go further, and test a bold tile design by laying out appropriately sized and colored pieces of paper to get a feel for the pattern in the actual space.

A horizontal or vertical thrust in an overall tile pattern carries the eye to visually lengthen a room or add needed height. Horizontal patterns, such as a backsplash border extending into a chair rail, tend to be more restful than vertical lines. Diagonal lines are dynamic, with a space-enhancing feeling of movement. Visually breaking up an area, such as inserting a few decorative tiles amid a long counter, makes a feature less monolithic and imposing.

THE SHAPE OF THINGS

In the overall layout, anything beyond the straight "jack-on-jack" grid of matching squares is instantly eye-catching. Even running the same grid diagonally has a more dynamic, space-enhancing effect. Here are a few more layout possibilities:

◆ Rows of large squares staggered with smaller inserts.

◆ Interlocking hexagons in a honeycomb style.

◆ A chevron pattern of paired parallelograms.

◆ Rectangles run in herringbone or basket weave.

◆ Elongated hexagons or "pickets" interlocked around squares.

◆ Large cut-corner squares inset with a small square "dot," sometimes in a contrasting color—presents a timeless look.

◆ Curvaceous interlocking ogee or Provençal shapes, which often lend an exotic flavor.

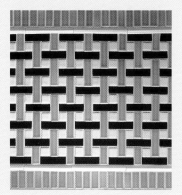

Clockwise from above: Even gentle natural tints command attention in imaginative patterns, such as a tiny square with subtle tonal shifts contained in sculpted trim, a serpentine mosaic border, and an eye-teasing basket weave.

SIZE MATTERS

Part of a pattern's character stems from its scale. Big tiles and big decorative patterns have more impact than smaller squares, which tend to read as a low-key texture. Generally, patterns are planned in proportion with the space: tiny designs may get lost, or grow "busy" or "spotty" in a big room. A bold pattern can overwhelm tight quarters, and an excessively big square can too clearly point out the room's shortcomings (and perhaps require lots of cut tiles and waste). But the rules are not absolute. A fairly big square reduces the number of grout lines for a sleeker, less busy appearance. And though mosaics are individually small, in contrasting colors they add up to a vigorous overall pattern that holds its own even in a cavernous room.

A subtler pattern derives from the mottling, highlights, and color variations of glazes, particularly hand-applied glazes. Unglazed tiles may have dark flashed streaks from mineral reactions in the clay, or shade from light to dark according to how close it was placed to the kiln's heat source. In the hands of a skillful installer, these random variations, laid down first in a dry run, can merge into an overall flow.

A far-stronger pattern is added with decorative tiles sporting pictures and designs. These can be scattered randomly or massed for a stronger effect into a border or a mural, which might be just a four-tile insert or a full, dazzling *trompe l'oeil* wall of flower-draped trellises.

Many tile patterns derive from nature: flowers, fruits and vegetables, and animals are enduring themes. More realistic renderings seem most at home in traditional rooms, while

stylized forms can span a wider decorative range. Abstract patterns can be time-honored motifs, such as a Greek scroll or Gothic fretwork or more idiosyncratic and modern. Regular, repeating patterns tend to be relaxing and carry the eye smoothly across the space while more unexpected ones are dynamic and eye-catching.

ON THE BORDER

A particularly useful category of decorative tile includes borders, sometimes called liners, feature strips, or listelli. These are generally longer and slimmer than the accompanying field tiles. Although many domestic and international manufacturers provide borders coordinated to the field tiles, you're not limited to these. The field tile itself can serve as a border. A row in a larger or smaller size, a different shape, a contrasting color, or a different angle, turned on its side for a run of diamonds edged in cut-tile triangles—any of these could be enough to frame an installation. Even tile from a different manufacturer can serve as a border, although any difference in thickness will need to be accommodated during installation.

A border eases the transition between materials, such as where tile meets plaster or one tile pattern meets another. A favorite effect is a chair rail separating plain-tiling above and a trellis-like diagonal layout on the wainscot. Breaking up the long stretches of tile can improve the perceived proportions. In a tiny, high-ceilinged bathroom, a picture-rail border visually lowers the ceiling to keep the space from feeling like an elevator shaft.

Dimensional borders, rope moldings, or hand-molded, high-relief trimmings break up the flat plane of tilework and strongly define a room without necessarily adding a lot of color. A brightly patterned border can balance a whole wall of plain squares, while a solid-color trim gives a clear, containing edge to a strong overall design. And you're not limited to one border: stacking several borders—such as a bold-relief egg-and-dart molding, a checkerboard feature strip echoing the field-tile colors, and a pencil-thin liner—could add up to a luxurious chair rail.

Doors, windows, fireplaces, and niches can be framed in decorative trim. For such wraparound treatments, decide how the border pattern will meet at the corners: whether

Opposite: In a moderate-size bath, the rich-hued tile wainscot, topped with a bold border, runs through the glassed shower stall for a longer continuous line.

Below: A bullnose molding, slim liner tiles, and a border in delicate relief are dramatic in form, yet neutral.

mitered, butted together, or separated with a corner block of tile or other material. The pattern should also look equally good running vertically and horizontally.

Because borders draw the eye so emphatically, they should seem logical, symmetrical, and centered in the space. Often a border is placed to continue another horizontal line, such as the top of the counter, or the soffit above the cabinets, for a coherent overall picture. Decorative details also gain from repetition. One little stretch of tiled border around a window might seem random. But picked up again in decorative inserts scattered on the floor, or on the backsplash, it becomes part of a theme.

TEXTURAL PLAYS

Texture is subtle, integral part of interior design, yet one easily overlooked in the early planning. A tile can have visual texture, with suggestions of depth from variations in the glaze and pattern, or a tactile surface with a gritty glaze or a sculptural design. The irregularities of handmade tile, or a commercial line with a handmade look, can be an unexpected yet satisfying textural note.

Smooth, high-gloss surfaces catch the light to enhance a feeling of space and make colors brighter and livelier. Such polished finishes tend to have a formal, deliberate, more dramatically

Above: Tile borders should make logical divisions in the space. These strong rows outline the counter and the privacy wall, and echo the tile-trimmed mirror.

"decorated" ambiance. More rugged, matte textures seem more casual and natural; they make the hues deeper and more solid, and tend to condense the space.

As in most aspects of decorating, texture gains from strategic contrast. In a room that's predominantly bright and glossy, a simple unglazed floor tile might add a grounding note. Juxtaposing matte and glossy tiles in the same color can lend a wonderful depth to a flat wall.

ULTIMATELY PRACTICAL

In the end, decorating decisions come back to their beginnings, with a final

check for the practical requirements. Does the manufacturer specify the tile as suitable for the intended purpose? Will it be easy care, particularly for high-use areas or floors that have outdoor access? Smooth, glossy glazed tiles are easy to wipe, but they tend to show every smudge. Conversely, matte unglazed tiles generally hold on to dirt, but don't show it as readily. Solid colors, particularly if very light and very dark, tend to show soil more easily than a mid-tone with a soft-edged, concealing pattern. Dark-glazed floor tiles tend to show wear more quickly than light finishes.

Professional decorators sometimes test the room's proposed balance by assembling a sample board, bringing together all the materials in the approximate proportions. The do-it-yourselfer needn't be so formal. Yet if you're facing a major renovation, you might want to gather samples of the intended tile and the rest of the room's ingredients, to assess the overall impression. Does it seem too of-a-piece and need some enlivening contrasts? Or does it seem jumbled and in need of editing? Looking at the total picture assures a harmonious whole, with the tilework playing its part.

Above: Variety in the colors and textures enlivens a Southwestern bath. Earthy terra-cotta contrasts with the glossy wall tiles and glass block; the wall's warm yellow finds a foil in the tile's equally rich shades of green.

CHAPTER 6

COOKING WITH TILE

Kitchen Concepts

Ceramic tile is a standard-issue kitchen surface, chosen for its ability to withstand heat, spatters, spills, smoke, and wear. Yet how often can you make such a sensible choice that still allows for luxury and endless design imagination? Properly chosen, tile can serve equally well on floors, walls, or counters. It can roll across wide expanses or provide the telling details.

The kitchen is the house's engine, where the business of daily life takes place. Beyond the general considerations of decorating with tile, examined in the previous chapter, a kitchen entails special concerns because of its central role.

In designing your kitchen, consider its full range of activities, beyond cooking and cleanup. It may also be where the kids do homework or happily mess with crafts, and where you balance the checkbook, work on your novel, or plan your schedule. Maybe it's an annex to a garden, subject to muddy feet, the repotting of geraniums, and piles of fresh produce.

Often the kitchen serves for family dining and lots of casual entertaining. Do you cook alone or with helpers and onlookers? Consider also how the kitchen relates to the adjoining spaces, such as a family room, patio, or home office. In a multipurpose great room, the same tile can easily shift gears between the utilitarian kitchen core and the adjoining family and entertainment space. Or if you prefer, a change of pattern or scale could signal the boundaries between each area.

STAR OR TEAM PLAYER

Regardless of your kitchen style, tile can be an understated backdrop or the room's showstopper. A busy kitchen chock full of countertop appliances, spice racks, and bright collectibles might need the visual relief of a neutral, textured tile. In a room with carved-and-fretted cabinets, a cathedral ceiling, and stunning windows, a bold tile pattern might be overkill, as the attention is pulled in too many directions.

Conversely, a streamlined kitchen, where the decks are cleared, might need the visual emphasis of decorative tile. In a small kitchen, where every inch has to function, tile can add color and pattern amid the workspaces without cluttering up shelves or counters.

Tile evokes a mood, whether as a sweet, hand-painted floral to accompany scrubbed-pine woodwork or buff-toned porcelain beneath slick Euro-style cabinetry. The kitchen is the traditional showcase for decorative tile. Consider how old Mediterranean country kitchens sometimes present a *mélange* of strong tile patterns added over generations, for an effect charmingly chaotic.

Even without that kind of pattern-on-pattern overload, a classic tile reproduction, with realistic fruits and vegetables, herbs and flowers, or lush Moorish arabesques, instantly layers on an old-world ambiance. More stylized relief-molded designs in richly glazed hues might serve for an Arts and

Crafts-style kitchen. Brisk geometric patterns, such as slim, lipstick-red accent tiles in a white backsplash, could add zest to a lean, modern setting.

Beyond such in-character choices, tile can also provide a piquant contrast: an earthy unglazed tile might keep ornate cabinetry from seeming too cute, while a backsplash glazed in a lustrous rose tint could charmingly counterpoint a minimalist modern space.

Above: An old-world mural beneath a classic mantel gives a massive, modern range a hearth-like warmth.

KITCHEN COLORS

Color is the music of decorating. We respond to the atmosphere created by particular colors. Because most households spend so much time in the kitchen, its color choices have to wear especially well. Reds and yellows, whether a backsplash decked in vibrant daffodils or, more softly, in an understated russet-hued quarry tile, play up the room's warmth and vitality. Such colors seem appetizing and hospitable in a room geared for eating and entertaining—that's why restaurant interiors tend to play up the warmer side of the spectrum.

Below: A random tile patchwork across the backsplash was inspired by the whimsically colorful mood of the owners' cookie jars.

But you may be drawn toward cool, serene blues and greens to counteract the heat of cooking and the bustle of activity. The room's natural light may influence color choices. A yellow wall might seem overwarm in a large-windowed, south-facing room, yet it could put a glow on a dark kitchen in a rainy climate.

Whenever possible, examine the tile samples in the kitchen's natural and artificial light at different times of the day. Many building codes now mandate that new kitchens and baths be fitted with energy-saving fluorescent fixtures. Traditional fluorescents were known for their cold, bluish light, which drabbed down reds and yellows and made skin tones look sallow. Today, fluorescents span a much wider category. Bulbs are rated by their

Left: A sharp checkerboard on a dynamic diagonal holds its own against the visual strength of bright yellow enameled walls and forest-green woodwork, adding up to a high-energy whole.

Below: A simple green back-splash and tiled counters in an understated white combine with matching woodwork for a soothing background.

Kelvin (K) color temperature, with, paradoxically, the lower K number numbers indicating a warmer illumination, ranging from a fairly cool 4,100K to a "deluxe warm-white" at 3,000K. More-expensive fluorescent bulbs, coated inside with rare earth phosphors, can be even more energy efficient and offer color rendition more closely approximating daylight.

The colors already on hand in kitchen cabinetry, display pieces, tableware, and china may affect the tile choices. Kitchens tend to be dynamic spaces, filled with the changing pieces of daily living. This undercuts the chances of maintaining a strict, dramatic color scheme as a set piece. Rather than meticulously matching everything, particularly across different materials, it's useful to consider a favorite color as a family of darker shades and lighter tints. Tile tints don't fade with sunlight, cleaning, or wear, so carefully coordinated curtains or seat cushions will tend to look less matched over the years anyway. Besides, you'll want to update those items.

Above: An irregular surface and a high-gloss glaze give a tactile appeal to the backsplash's easy-to-live-with neutral tone.

Left: Behind the range, a bold frame of border tiles brings focus to expanses of creamy tiles set on a jazzy diagonal.

Left: In a turn-of-the-century house, the white, brick-like "subway" tile and the hexagonal mosaic floor, factory-mounted with a classic design, have a suitably nostalgic feel.

Below: The white surfaces play up the kitchen's lofty expanses and emphasize the deep, arched niche that hides the professional range's ventilation equipment.

White is the perennial choice for kitchens because it connotes a fresh cleanliness and visually expands a well-filled room. These qualities play to particular advantage in a small, functional room since expanses of white in a big kitchen might seem too surgical or glaringly bright. Big or small, a white kitchen demands meticulous housekeeping, even with a low-maintenance ceramic surface. White and light colors also help achieve the high illumination levels needed in a working kitchen. Dark finishes will demand higher-key lighting.

Neutral But Noteworthy

In mixable, easygoing tones of white, these kitchens show their more stylish side with adventurous choices of shape, texture, and scale.

TYPES OF APPLICATIONS

The range of ways to use tile extends only as far as the homeowner's or designer's imagination. Tile lends itself to many areas from floors and counters to backsplashes and walls—and in some cases even ceilings.

UNDERFOOT IN THE KITCHEN

Tile can be a practical, easy-to-keep, long-lasting floor, but as with any flooring choice, it has its disadvantages. If you stroll barefoot, tile can feel unpleasantly cold and hard, and it can be tiring to stand on. It's also merciless on every dropped plate and glass. A preponderance of hard surfaces in a room magnifies voices and appliance noise, a special concern if the kitchen opens to other living spaces.

To bear up to kitchen traffic, tiled floors should be unglazed with a non-wear surface or glazed with a Porcelain Enamel Institute (PEI) rating of Class III or IV, designated for medium- and heavy-use floors. A room with outdoor access, subject to abrasive, tracked-in dirt, needs a particularly durable floor. Amid a kitchen's greasy spills, a nonslip surface is vital. But be wary of extremely gritty textures or dimensional patterns that can trap dirt. Rustic "pillowed" tiles with eased-down edges must be carefully rinsed, as wash-water can pool in low, wide grout lines and leave a grimy residue. Except for impervious porcelain tile and smooth, dense epoxy grouts, most unglazed products and grout lines should be sealed against kitchen stains and resealed periodically.

Dark, glossy glazes tend to show wear more quickly than light-colored finishes, though a very light floor, especially in a solid color, may be too much work to maintain. A mid-tone color choice with some concealing pattern is probably easiest to keep. A black-and-white checkerboard floor, though a smashing look, highlights both light and dark smudges.

The tile and any new substrate will raise the floor's height. In new construction, a tiled floor is often laid across the

whole empty space, under cabinetry and appliances. This protects the subfloor and readies the room for possible changes should a cabinet be removed or a peninsula added. In a renovation, a new tile floor generally ends at the front edge of the existing cabinetry. Make sure, however, that any slide-in appliances can still be pulled forward for repairs.

COMFORT STRATEGIES

Tile's unyielding surface is hard on the feet and echoes any kitchen noise. There are, however, strategies for downplaying such drawbacks:

◆ Add cushioned, nonslip rugs in front of the sink and the main food-prep counter to make a tiled floor easier on the legs.

◆ In new construction or major renovation, consider radiant in-floor heating systems to give a gentle warmth to a tiled floor. Older systems carried warmed water through copper pipes embedded in the subfloor. Newer systems use durable polymer tubing; newer still are thin networks of metal coils embedded in thinset mortar.

◆ Plan ahead for sound control by choosing appliances rated for quiet operation and including some plush fabrics, seat cushions, rugs, and pillows wherever possible.

Left: Ebullient turquoise and white squares take part in the fun of this stainless-steel kitchen, which harks back to 1950s diners. Such glossy surfaces, with white tile underfoot, require careful maintenance to keep that glittering retro look.

COUNTER PROPOSALS

Opinions differ dramatically on ceramic tile applied to countertops. Some homeowners and designers shy away from the uneven surface and the potential maintenance problems with the grout lines. Yet in regions with a heritage in tile, it's a common countertop choice. Many homeowners love the look of tile and the design possibilities of its tough, heat-proof surface.

Technical problems can be minimized by discussing the project with a knowledgeable salesperson and by choosing sturdy tile rated for countertop use. As with flooring, a smooth, matte tile with a narrow, flush-to-the-surface grout line is easiest to clean. A larger tile minimizes the number of grout lines, which become even less of a bugaboo with latex-enhanced cement grout and a quality sealer or with impervious epoxy formulations. Some grouts and sealers are not recommended for use around food.

To protect tile in daily use, clean up spills promptly, especially acidic foods such as lemon juice and vinaigrette, which can mar some glazes. Avoid cutting on the ceramic surface, which may scratch the tile and dull the knife.

An existing laminate, stone, or tile counter, if flat and sturdy, can serve as a substrate for new tilework. More often, the old counter is removed and replaced with 3/4-inch exterior plywood screwed to the cabinet base and braced from below to prevent flexing. On a sink counter, the plywood may be covered with water-resistant cement backer board.

Above: Heat-proof tile inserted in a butcher-block counter demonstrates a strategic mix of materials.
Below: Tiled counters are easy-to-clean cool surfaces for baking areas.

Tile can also put a company face on a counter ledge that doubles for casual snack and buffet serving. Such overhangs must be well supported to avoid flexing. If the cabinet wall in front of the counter stools gets kicked and scuffed, tile it, too. A pass-through window to the dining room or family room also benefits from a dressing of tile, perhaps relating to a decorative motif in the adjoining space.

Edge Treatments. Counter edges are finished in a variety of ways, beginning with a simple bullnose tile overlapping a narrow, vertical sidepiece. The most common edge treatment is a one-piece, V-cap trim tile that wraps over the side. Often such trim has a bumped-up edge to contain spills, though some designers find such trim to be visually heavy.

Dimensional ceramic moldings or wood trim can

Opposite: A rounded bullnose tile in crisp black-and-white and dashes of vivid colors give an extra visual bounce to the kitchen's cool geometric forms.

also handsomely finish off the counter's edge. Wood, however, expands and contracts with changes in temperature and moisture. Even with flexible setting materials, a wood trim on tile is subject to water damage and crumb-collecting gaps. Counter tiles can also be mitered at the edges for a crisp, precise look (but one prone to chipping). Because counters jut out near the level of an adult's hips or a child's head, avoid sharp outside corners.

Around Sinks. More than half of kitchen work involves the sink, where most cooking tasks begin and end. Because this feature is so prominent, it should fall gracefully in tile layout, framed either in full tiles or cut tiles carefully matched on either side.

Top-mounted, or *self-rimming*, sinks of steel or porcelain are the easiest to install in a tiled counter. The outer, splash-containing lip of the drop-in unit sits on top of the surrounding tile and is sealed with a bead of flexible, water-proof caulk. An *undermounted* sink, by contrast, is clipped to the underside of the counter opening. Convex trim tiles, cut to fit, cover the gap between the sink and the exposed tile edges. This custom-fitted finish, though attractive, is more expensive, and its multiple seams are more vulnerable to water infiltration.

Using waterproof setting materials, a skilled installer can even create the whole sink in tile, though probably one more suitable as an eye-catching bar sink than the main kitchen work center.

In today's kitchen designs, countertop materials are sometimes strategically combined. Tile might fashion a decorative backsplash above a stone-slab counter or be inserted in a laminate counter as a heatproof "landing strip" near the oven or rangetop. On a big island or other large workspaces, a tiled design can effectively break up and give a stylish variety to what otherwise would be a bulky expanse.

Above: Rustic tilework in a rich gold with a heavy V-cap edge creates a countertop with a rugged, folky flavor and an appealing simplicity.
Left: An undermounted sink, finished with a rim of convex trim tiles, melds smoothly into place.

SPLASHY POSSIBILITIES

The backsplash wall between the counters and cabinets gives decorative tilework maximum visibility. In an area with a vertical height of only about 18 inches, even a few special tiles scattered in the field make an impression. Sometimes the backsplash is just one row of tiles at the back of the counter. But a fully tiled backsplash is more easily kept and is more resistant to heat and wetness. Inserting a concave cove trim where the wall meets the counter creates a smoothly rounded, easy-to-wipe joint rather than a sharp crevice.

A large-scale tilework design or mural, like a painting, needs enough room to be seen. If your counters brim with appliances, canisters, racks and fruit bowls, a scattered design or a

Above: A mural of hand-painted poultry nests on the tiled backsplash of a spacious country kitchen. Bold pictorial effects work best in a large space, where the whole can be appreciated.

Above: Turning simple squares on the diagonal makes them into an eye-catching two-tone harlequin pattern, carefully laid out to symmetrically frame the window. The tile's warm natural colors complement the mid-toned woodwork.

repeating border, placed fairly high, might come across better than a scenic design where the whole must be appreciated. Consider also the likely viewing angle: in a narrow galley kitchen, the top of a full-height design is obscured by the angle of the cabinets, while one facing out to a dining area is more completely on display.

Electrical outlets are often annoyingly scarce in older kitchens. If your renovation includes new electrical outlets in the backsplash, plan their placement as part of the tile design, whether they sit above the backsplash or tiles are cut to fit around them. Local building codes may also have something to say about their positioning. If you're having tile custom-made for the backsplash, a ceramic faceplate might be made to match. If the outlets intrude too much on the tilework design, consider concealing them underneath the cabinets.

Undercabinet lights, whether mini-fluorescents or miniature track fixtures, illuminate the work counters and spotlight the backsplashes. Such fixtures should be mounted close to

Right: Multicolor, high-contrast squares, recalling modern paintings, complement the lean, simple cabinetry. Though seemingly random, such patterns should be carefully worked out beforehand to balance the pattern's elements.

the front of cabinets to minimize glare and to avoid "wall-washing," a downward play of light that creates shadows by exaggerating the normal unevenness of a tiled wall.

The backsplash behind the sink or the rangetop, where the upper cabinets are usually shortened or nonexistent, is a natural focal point for decorative tilework. A fireproof, nonabsorbent backing such as tile is especially essential behind high-powered professional cooking equipment and messy indoor grills. Beautiful, tactile designs molded in high relief do have more nooks and crannies to keep clean in a splatter-prone spot. But such a showcase spot for a unique tile may be worth a little extra maintenance.

Above: An adobe-like stucco arch forms an attractive range hood. Tile with a handmade look completes the rustic ambiance.

The range, particularly a massive model, can be framed in a tile-clad alcove, which conceals the requisite ventilation system. Or just the backsplash can be tiled and the range hood trimmed in decorative tile. Each gives a more hearth-like presence, a particularly appealing touch in a country kitchen evoking Tuscany or Mexico. Prefabricated hoods of thin sheet metal are too flexible to support tile. A custom hood can be made in heavy-gauge steel or of wood framing covered in plywood and cement backer board. Adhesives and grouts must be heat resistant.

Small touches of tile have a charm all their own in a kitchen design and may be particularly effective if repeated in several different ways.

Above: Consider tucking in a pot of flowers that you never have to worry about watering!

◆ If a full wainscot is beyond your plans, a molding tile can serve as a chair rail. One row of bullnose tiles also makes a charming baseboard.

◆ Tile can enliven the interior of a glass-fronted cabinet or can be a decorative medallion on a solid cabinet door.

◆ A shallow storage niche for small spice bottles, teacups, candlesticks, or knickknacks can be created between the studs and clad in decorative tile. Glass or wire shelves let more of the decoration shine through.

◆ Tile can brighten the area between the ceiling beams of a country kitchen or can put a pretty border on a projecting soffit.

◆ Windows and doorways can be framed in tile. Ceramic can waterproof the floor of a flower-filled greenhouse window.

◆ Decorative tile can extend to the furniture, adding a durable top to a table or serving credenza or a handsome back wall to a breakfront hutch. An added advantage: such pieces of decorative tilework may someday move with you to brighten another kitchen.

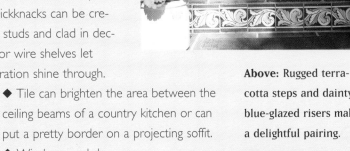
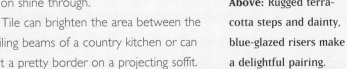

Above: Rugged terracotta steps and dainty, blue-glazed risers make a delightful pairing.

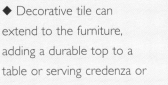
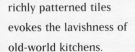

Above: A wraparound of richly patterned tiles evokes the lavishness of old-world kitchens.

Right: Classic tile motifs add a historical touch.

TILE IN THE BATH

Beyond the Basics

A little more than a century ago, just possessing a separate, plumbed-in bathroom was considered luxurious. But in our day, we expect that utility to be delivered with a certain amount of style—a dual goal admirably served by ceramic tile. It bears up to moisture and steady use, and, in a room where hygiene is paramount, it is nonabsorbent and easy to clean. Bathrooms are generally small, packed with essential, standardized equipment, and short on elaborate furnishings or window treatments. Tile often steps into the spotlight as the room's decorative star.

THE BIG PICTURE

Finishing materials, such as tile, must wait until all decisions are made concerning plumbing, structural, and electrical work. A major renovation might involve reconfiguring the floor plan, taking into account local building codes, which specify minimum clearances between the fixtures. A well-planned layout, essential for smooth functioning within limited dimensions, will also determine if there's floor space for an elegant "area rug" of tile, or enough wall space to show a mural to advantage. The floor plan also suggests the natural focal points where the eye will fall.

Often bath remodeling aims to open up the room by incorporating some adjoining area, adding windows and skylights, or removing obstructions. But sometimes a large family bathroom becomes more useful with privacy dividers, additions that can be gracefully integrated with tilework.

Above: A spacious master bath allows scope for a tiled "area rug" in warm terra-cotta tones.

Previous pages: Framed in boldly dimensional rope-molding trim tiles, a composition of varied shapes and soft hues makes a tub-side centerpiece.

Beyond the general decorating principles discussed in Chapter 5 (pages 66-83), think of the ways tile can advance your design goals. A master bath might be planned as a soothing retreat, highlighted by a large soaking tub and such luxuries as a dressing area, a makeup table, an exercise corner, or a private terrace. A chosen tile could unify the different areas or link the bath to the master bedroom's color scheme.

A bathroom shared by several siblings may require especially sturdy tilework, maybe decorated with a bit of whimsy. Tile lasts longer than fleeting childhood, however, so be wary of cute juvenile tile patterns unless you're prepared for additional renovations—or additional children—down the line. A first-floor powder room might feature more-delicate decorative ceramics than a much-used family bathroom that hosts steady traffic and several steamy showers every morning.

Bathroom floors are generally less abused than their kitchen counterparts, so durability ratings are less crucial. In a bathroom, subject only to light "slipper traffic" off a bedroom, wall tiles could even suffice. However, because household situations can change, it's best to err on the side of too sturdy a finish.

Above: Tile's versatility lets it frame the mirror and clad the countertop in bouncy geometric patterns of rose and blue.

HEALTH AND SAFETY

Unchecked moisture can loosen tile, cause allergenic, unattractive molds and mildew, and work through to underlying structures. So an essential, if unglamorous, aspect of designing with tile is ensuring adequate ventilation, which is most effectively installed before the finishing work. An exhaust system should be placed close to the shower and bath, mounted high on an outside wall between the studs or in between the ceiling joists, with ducts running horizontally to the wall or up to a roof vent. Local building codes may also dictate duct placement. Fans are rated in cubic feet per minute (CFM). Follow the manufacturer's recommendations in sizing the unit. Noise levels are stated in sones. The higher the number, the louder the unit. A quiet-running system with an automatic shutoff is more likely to be used consistently.

For all their air of peaceful repose, bathrooms can be hazardous, combining awkwardly tight spaces and smooth, wet surfaces. Floor tiles must be slip-resistant, as specified in manufacturers' product literature. Most unglazed tiles provide a reasonably good grip (although some sealers will undermine this quality), as does the pebbled surface of mosaics. Glazed tiles with an added texture or grit, or the slightly wavy profile of a floor-rated handmade tile, may provide the needed traction.

Will the room be used by children (even visiting ones) or anyone with disabilities? Bear in mind that physical capabilities can change at any time. Thus, a room with unnecessary changes in level, a sunken bathtub, or slick floors, however visually dramatic, may be less desirable as time goes on, or limit the potential buyers at resale time.

Even for the most able-bodied, the bathroom is a prime site for household accidents and falls. The path to the toilet, sometimes sleepily traversed in the dark of night, should be unobstructed and without changes in level. In the shower or tub areas, protruding soap dishes and towel bars adhered only with a thin layer of adhesive will not support you in a fall. Consider adding weight-bearing grab bars, now available in snazzier, less-institutional styling. Grab bars are easily bolted to the wall studs before the tiling is done but are more troublesome to add later as a retrofit.

Above: Two-inch squares in a diagonal array put a strong border on the bath, contrasting with an oversize checkerboard on the tub platform. **Opposite:** Modular tiles in graduated sizes scatter the room with lively rectilinear designs, echoing the glass-block bay window. **Left:** In the separate shower, the same tiles frame a niche for the toiletries.

Stepped-up tub platforms can be beautifully arrayed in tile but should also be planned for safe use. The bather should be able to enter and leave the tub without being tipped dangerously off balance. Some deep tubs are raised in the platform high enough so that the user can sit down on the edge and swing his legs over to enter the tub safely. Any steps around a tub should be skid-proof and very slightly sloped so that water doesn't pool there.

DESIGNED FOR PLEASURE

Once the practical demands are considered, let your imagination move on to how tile might express the intended mood of this private space. Maybe you envision a clean, healing spa-like atmosphere with a simple grid of cool colors and lean, unfussy outlines. Or maybe you're aiming for a sense of hedonistic luxury, with lushly ornamental patterns in glossy finishes or opulent hand-applied glazes. Or a restful mood with large, satin-finished squares in dreamy pastels. Or a cheery family bathroom, bright with simple geometric borders. Visions of long, lingering baths are appealing, but for most households the bathroom is a short-stay space. Thus, it can carry off a more dramatic treatment that might grow tiresome in a kitchen, where long hours are spent.

Below left: Tile sets the stylistic pace, giving an old fashioned flavor to a fully equipped modern bathroom with a wainscot of delft-like blue-and-white florals.
Below right: A bold geometric border reminiscent of a cozy country quilt warms an all-white scheme.

Decorative tilework can also reflect a home's period flavor—even if it harks back to an era before a bathroom was standard equipment. Charming delftware designs or calico-like prints might suit a classic Colonial, just as boldly handcrafted Arts and Crafts motifs are at home in a turn-of-the-century bungalow or country florals in a summer cottage. Aquatic images of fish, waves, and seashells are also frequently invoked for baths.

In what's usually a small room, patterns are generally kept in scale, though the bathroom's dimensions will make a bold decorative stroke, such as a sweeping geometric patchwork, seem even bolder. In this context, a few special, possibly handcrafted tiles, make a strong statement. Mass-produced tiles also present rich possibilities because they often provide such fine color gradations, as well as modular sizes to interlock into an overall design.

Mosaics are a lively, textural finish that can trace curves and columns, and even the outside of a freestanding tub. Commercially made 1-inch porcelain tiles in circular "pennies," squares, or hexagons have a nostalgic aura and can be special-ordered from the factory in custom designs for today's vintage-look baths.

Even more personalized and colorful finishes come from the hands of mosaic artists creating free-form designs that incorporate tiles and tile shards of varied shapes and sizes, sometimes mixed with bits of broken plate, stone, seashells, or glass. Such precise, on-site artistry is extremely expensive. Preassembled art mosaics, sometimes in custom designs, are also available premounted onto mesh. They may be sized to drop into a field of standard 4-inch wall

Above: A pointillist artwork, this modernistic bathroom is streamlined and simple but pops with a full wraparound of multihued mosaics.

Left: "Pique-assiette," or "broken-dish," mosaicwork creates one-of-a-kind compositions with random bits of china and such.

Below: A mix of sizes can also create drama, as in a bathroom with boldly oversize squares on the floors and delicately dimensional borders.

Opposite: Even standard 4-inch bathroom squares, available in a versatile color range, can be inspiring when set into a bold patchwork.

tiles, replacing one, two, four, or more squares, to be scattered in the field or massed into a larger mural. In any mosaic, the choice of grout color and texture is integral to the design.

A tiled border can frame important features or emphasize the room's horizontal or vertical dimensions. Such strong trim should run logically and symmetrically, since the bathroom will be taken in at a glance. Align decorative tiles and murals to reflect in a mirror, and you can double their impact at no added cost. Multilayer borders combining narrow decorative strips, thick cornices, and slim liner tiles are displayed to advantage at chair-rail height.

COLOR CUES

Color choices immediately create ambience. In a bathroom, warm hues are comfortable and enclosing, and rosy tints, such as coral or peach, are flattering to skin tones. Blues and greens carry connotations of cool, refreshing waters and airy natural settings.

Deep-toned, glossy tilework, though dramatic in a company powder room, will show every soap streak and smudge in a heavily used space. Dark colors, particularly in matte finishes, tend to advance visually, to bring down a high ceiling or make a cavernous master bath more intimate. Sometimes the aim is a cozy "jewel box" filled with rich hues and tactile finishes, though intense colors are generally reserved for accents or for less-permanent elements. Dark surroundings also demand stronger task lighting for a room where you shave, apply makeup, or remove splinters.

Left: Wide grout lines and tiles with a "pillowed" profile give sand-tinted walls an intriguing texture. The clear-glass shower stall, though requiring extra upkeep, opens up the space and shows off the subtle tile. Dimensional moldings edge the tub with yet another tactile accent.

More often the goal is to enhance the sense of space, usually with a flow of light tints, made brighter and sleeker with a glossy finish. Using the same tile, perhaps in a different size, for both floor and walls unifies the room; a coordinated series of floor, wall, and trim tiles will likewise carry the eye smoothly. Another unifying touch is color-matching the fixtures with the tile, a job made easier by cooperation among major manufacturers. The hands-down favorite in both product categories, however, continues to be white.

Right: Softly mottled to suggest marble blocks, these tiled shower walls seem even more classic with a mosaic border topped in elegant dentil moldings.

Left: Wainscots of creamy-hued rectangles laid in staggered brick-like formation seem slightly antique and completely at home with the wallpaper's strong scenic-toile design.

Below: Heavy moldings and panels of diagonal tiles layer the traditional room with fine details.

Right: By repeating the decorative tile moldings throughout the large bathroom, the designer unifies its different functional areas.

Tile can also be mixed to dramatic effect in a bath design, incorporating other hard materials such as solid surfacing, glass block, or stone, for an appealing textural contrast. Wood used in wet areas must be well sealed against moisture, making it a problematic edging for tile.

WET WALLS

In many bathrooms, the three walls framing the built-in tub showcase the most decorative tilework. The tile may extend to the ceiling, as is common in Europe, or just above the showerhead, often leading down to a wainscot around the room. In a room with a separate shower, where the alcove is for bathing only, the tile may extend only a few rows above the tub.

The standard built-in bathtub is unfinished on the three walled-in sides, with a front apron on the fourth. The tub apron can also be replaced or covered with a tiled panel, either as a space-enhancing continuation of the floor or as a place for embellishment.

Many tub alcoves do double duty as the shower stall, enclosed by a shower curtain or translucent or clear safety-glass doors. These doors increase a feeling of space and show off

Below: Hand-painted tiles installed at eye level show a custom tile used sparingly yet effectively.

the tilework within. They do, however, require more maintenance to remain attractively crystal clear.

Another common tub style is the drop-in model, unfinished on all sides, ready to be set into a custom-built platform, surrounded by a handy ledge for books and toiletries. This is a common format for an oversize whirlpool tub. These may seem *de rigueur* in upscale master baths, but don't be swayed by fashion if you're strictly a shower-and-go type. Water-resistant tile is the standard decorative finish for such platforms. The tilework is usually fitted with an unobtrusive removable panel to gain access to the pump motors.

A platform tub is usually paired with a separate shower, another potential decorative tile display. To fend off the condensed moisture of a steamy shower, tile may even extend across the shower ceiling, often set on the diagonal to avoid conflict with the sidewall's pattern. Some custom showers are designed with an open configuration—an elegant version of a locker room—or with the spray facing away from the opening. Most standard shower stalls, however, require the choice of a curtain or door.

Underfoot, a professional installer can custom-craft a tiled shower floor with nonslip vitreous tile or mosaics set in a mud-bed of mortar, gently sloped toward the drain.

Above: A bold trim tile frames the tub niche in a graceful arch, to contrast with the right-angled two-tone border.

More often, the shower pan is a prefabricated molded unit.

Shower and tub walls require careful waterproofing. Ideally, the tile would be highly impervious to moisture. But the lightweight, easy-to-cut clay bodies of most wall tiles are actually fairly absorbent. They rely on the impenetrable glazed surface and water-resistant setting materials to succeed in this demanding installation. Ordinary drywall disintegrates when wet, so the standard for bathroom installations around the tub and shower is a water-resistant version called green board or blue board. The better substrate in tub and shower areas is cement-and-glass-mesh backer board, which remains rigid even when wet. The seams between the boards should be sealed with fiberglass tape and surfaced with tile adhesive or mortar.

Accessories. Some wall-tile collections extend to coordinating ceramic accessories, soap dishes, towel bars and hooks, cup and toothbrush holders, and perhaps a handpainted sink.

Top: Walls patterned in fine pinstripes and a niche of squares-within-a-square play with tile's geometry.
Above: Another example of handy storage emphasized with tile patterns, these recessed shelves juxtapose diagonals, straight lines, and rounded trims.
Right: Going far beyond the expected square are these custom-made ceramic swirls and interlocked triangles.

Stock ceramic accessories are also available in neutral colors. Some designers prefer to blend such necessities into the field-tile color, while others see them as "jewelry" that can perhaps pick up the color of the decorative motifs. The exact placement of these details should be planned beforehand, even though they're generally inserted last, sometimes with an extra-strong epoxy adhesive, into the opening left amid the installed tiles. Tile can also finish and integrate such useful architectural features as shower benches, storage ledges, shelves, and niches.

Care and Sealing. Grout lines around the tub or shower were traditionally maintenance headaches. Grout technology has advanced with mildew-resistant additives and dense, impervious latex-

Above: Tile can build useful architectural features, such as a deep tub-side window ledge for collectibles and toiletries. The varied sizes and patterns unite in gentle white and gray.

modified or epoxy surfaces that don't readily absorb the fungus-feeding moisture. Severe mildew problems might also suggest a moisture problem behind the wall, which surface scrubbing won't remedy. (See Chapter 10, pages 158-163.)

Cement-based grouts may require sealers, as recommended by the manufacturer. Using larger tiles with narrow spacing also minimizes the actual grout area. At trouble spots such as the tub line and the floor joint, where water collects in sharp corners, curved cove tiles can slough off the wetness.

SPLASHY SINKS

The bathroom sink (or lavatory, as design professionals say) tends to be another strong focal point. A pedestal or wall-mounted sink is visually light and space enhancing and opens up more of the wall to array with tile. While freestanding sinks usually have an integral, molded backsplash, the wall is often tiled for extra protection.

Vanities. A vanity can easily stow bathroom clutter and conceal electrical outlets, which otherwise need to be

Counter Proposals
Bathroom counters don't have much square footage, so they can be dressed up with just a few very special examples of ceramic art.

Above: Eight handcrafted squares add up to a unique bathroom with a whimsical Wild West theme.
Above right: A custom-glazed lavatory meets its match in a surrounding rainbow of tile.
Right: A drop-in sink has an overhanging lip that installs neatly over tile.

integrated into the tile design. This storage piece does take up more of the floor and wall, but it opens opportunities for an attractively tiled countertop. While the situation isn't as demanding or abrasion-prone as a kitchen workspace, a bathroom countertop tile should be resistant to the acids and chemicals found in harsh cleansers or such spills as alcohol or nail-polish remover.

Basins. Bathroom countertop sinks, like kitchen versions, divide into broad basic categories. The easiest to install is a self-rimming *top-mounted* sink, which is dropped into an opening in the counter, supported by its flanged lip, and sealed with a bead of adhesive caulk. *Flush-mounted* sinks meet evenly with the counter under a framing metal band. They're prone to

Above: An undermounted sink makes use of a circle of narrow-cut trim tiles to smooth the edges and add a touch of custom detail.

water infiltration and trapped dirt and are less often seen in new baths. *Undermounted* styles, clipped beneath the counter, are somewhat more practical for lighter bathroom use than tough kitchen duty. Quarter-round trim tiles, cut in narrow sections, may cover the joint between counter and sink with a custom edging.

Such details play up the unique nature of ceramic tile. Applied piece by piece, it allows for individual variation along the way. Yet those pieces can add up to a harmonious whole that gives a room, even the utilitarian bathroom, a sense of distinction.

CHAPTER 8

TILE UNBOUND

All Around the House

In the kitchen or bath, tile is an expected choice. Yet as part of tile's renaissance in recent decades, American homeowners have discovered its fresh decorative potential for rooms throughout the house. Entryways, living and family rooms, sun rooms, bedrooms, fireplaces, wainscots, staircases, and even furniture—all can be beautifully and durably finished in ceramics.

Tile flows easily between living spaces, linking kitchen with dining room, breeze-way with family room, bedroom with private terrace. With its piecework nature, it can run in broad planes of subtle texture or add just an accent, delicate or

Previous pages: Tile can underpin a house's character. Large squares of earthy terra-cotta suit the massive scale and rugged texture of a rambling log cabin.

Below: Glossier tile in a crisp two-tone composition shares in the cool geometry of a contemporary home.

dazzling. Sometimes such treatments suggest old-world traditions because in many European countries tile has long been used as part of the basic decorating vocabulary. But tile can be idiosyncratically modern, particularly when used in less-expected ways.

Tile also answers modern concerns about indoor air quality in tightly sealed homes. Made from natural materials and fired to an inert, fused state, ceramic tile can't release potential pollutants or produce dangerous fumes in a fire. It's also a nonallergenic surface that won't absorb pollen, dust, mold, or fumes, and can generally be maintained with simple, water-based cleaners. Allergy-prone households often eschew dust-catching curtains and clutter, so tile's decorative options might be particularly appreciated. In hot climates, ceramic's inherent coolness has always been an advantage. In chillier regions, an in-floor heating system, or at least some strategically placed rugs, may make tile more acceptable for bedrooms and general living space.

GRAND ENTRANCES

First impressions are important. The house's entryway opens up your private space to the outside world. It should extend a sense of welcome and suggest the flavor of the house beyond. Yet the entryway is hardly a place for fussy, delicate decorating. Tile used underfoot must be rated for heavy-duty use and slip-resistance, ready to face high traffic, wet boots, and abrasive tracked-in dirt. Even the walls, particularly if fitted with coat hooks and catchall shelves, must bear up to dripping coats and umbrellas, and hard knocks from bulky deliveries, swinging backpacks, and briefcases.

The entry foyer is often small, little more than a corridor. But because the entry is used so briefly, the emphasis is rarely on making the space seem bigger, and the pale, unified, glossy surfaces often employed for such illusions are less practical in such a demanding setting. In fact, an entry that feels warm and cozy, with rich colors and strong details, can make adjoining spaces, by contrast, feel more expansive. And because the viewers are just passing through, the design may lean toward the dramatic.

Pattern and Texture. Because most entryways hold minimal furniture, the patterns and textures of the finishes carry much of the decorative weight. Deep, earthy hues of

unglazed terra-cotta, quarry, and porcelain tiles can solidly underpin an entry foyer in a traditional home, as can glazed tiles that effectively mimic stone. Multi-toned effects in complex patterns, perhaps dizzying in larger doses, are perennial choices for entryways, stretching back to the striking black-and-white checkerboards of Renaissance villas. At the turn of the century, patterned encaustic tiles, multihued mosaics, or geometric patchworks of tiles enlivened many front halls. In some Mediterranean cultures, a mosaic-like "rug" of broken tiles is said to bar bad luck at the door. Despite their history, stone-like finishes and crisp geometric designs are equally suitable to contemporary homes.

A tiled wainscot is a practical and gracious finish to an entry hall, perhaps with large-scale squares, a diagonal layout, or unusual interlocking shapes. Tiles of lush, matte hues or faux stone finishes, topped with a heavy rolled molding or an intricate decorative border, make such a treatment less kitchen-like. A mirror is handy for a final check when heading out the front door, and a framework of tile makes this light-enhancing feature a decorative standout. A larger entry hall might even present an opportunity for a full wall of bright decorative tile or a hand-painted mural—artwork on the wall that never needs straightening.

Above left: Oversize tiles glazed in matte, softly variegated natural tints emphasize an entry hall's calm grandeur.
Above right: Catching the light from the clerestory windows and glass-framed doorway, a brown-and-white marble checkerboard adds a classical glow to an art-filled foyer.

WALL WORKS

In the seventeenth century, Dutch merchants started tiling
their walls to make bright, cheery interiors, and in the
eighteenth century, delicate hand-painted tiles were part of
many neoclassical manor houses. But in our own day, tiling a
wall or part of a wall in a general living space usually requires
special, decorative choices to override the material's kitchen-
and-bath connotation. Luckily the market is rife with possibilities—earthy squares with a handmade look for a rugged
wainscot, dimensionally embossed tiles to make an eye-
catching baseboard, or brightly glazed designs to create a
chair rail with hint of Morocco.

Windows and Doors. Tile can be used to highlight
windows and doorways. In new construction, a frame of
decorative squares embedded in the plaster can sit smoothly
flush with the finished wall, lending distinction to these features. Or the tile can trace the
existing moldings, perhaps moved out a strategic inch or two to avoid having to cut tiles.

Specific windowsill trim tiles are sometimes available with neatly rounded edges, making
a waterproof, easily cleaned spot for flowerpots. Pastel, glossy tile on window recesses
enhances the natural light. With a decoratively tiled window, other dressing may be minimal
— perhaps just a simple shade for light control.

Wainscots and Chair Rails. These features add charming detail with a traditional feeling,
with tile standing in for the expected wallpaper or wooden beadboard. Because the exact
height of the wainscot can vary from about 32 to 36 inches, it can be adjusted to the size of
the tile. In the Arts and Crafts era, wainscots were generally higher, though this style might
loom a bit large in a small room of standard height.

The top of the wainscot, so prominently on view, deserves some special treatment. This
might consist of a row of decorative tiles topped with a dimensional molding or just the field
tile turned at an angle or interspersed with a contrasting color. Or the lush tile molding can
be added by itself as the chair rail, perhaps repeated elsewhere in the room for continuity. If
you have a row of special tiles, such as custom-made or antique ones, they can be applied to
a plywood backing and edged with wood moldings and attached to the wall for a chair rail
that you can remove if you redecorate. Baseboards are generally inconspicuous, so a dramatic,
tiled version is attention getting, particularly if strongly patterned. A tall baseboard matched to
the tile underfoot, however, can foster the illusion of greater floor space.

Opposite: California's
Adamson House, a tile
museum on the grounds of
the old Malibu Potteries,
showcases a bold approach
to mixing patterns. Above
the elaborate wainscot,
a colorful mural opens
up a windowless nook.
Above: In another corner,
the baseboards and a
window frame present
undulating lines of exotic
Moorish patterns.

ON THE FLOOR

Beyond the kitchen and bath, tile appears most often on the floor. For design inspirations, look to Mediterranean interiors of Spain, Italy, southern France, and North Africa, where such treatments have long been the norm. Simple unglazed floor tiles or easy-care glazed squares in mellow hues can flow elegantly throughout an open floor plan and provide an understated backdrop to strongly patterned rugs, either modern or traditional. A very clean-edged, machine-modern tile may be softened with a few low-key area rugs, while a neutral clay-colored terra-cotta may be a foil for brighter bits of carpet. A combination of shapes, such as a cut-corner square inset with a tiny "dot" or rectangles laid into a her-ringbone or picket pattern, can vary the floor without adding more color. Unlike carpeting or wood, tile will not fade in sunlight or reveal where furniture has been moved.

Left: Taking inspiration both from the ceramics and the textiles of the Middle East, this intricate faux rug, detailed to the fringe, is brilliant underfoot in an Adamson House hallway.

Ceramics can create witty *trompe l'oeil* "area rugs" of their own. Several art potteries offer tile designs that replicate intricate Oriental-rug patterns, right down to trim patterned with fringe. Or you can create your own rug with tiles of contrasting colors and a mixture of sizes, carefully worked out on graph paper. Such *faux* rugs could serve as a nonslip runner in a hallway or be the living room's centerpiece.

Family Rooms. Family rooms generally see hard wear and often adjoin the kitchen, which provides plenty of messy snacks. So installing an easy-care tile, set with a high, flush grout line, is a good precaution. The floor may be kept neutral to accommodate changing accessories and to promote an atmosphere of calm. Or you might decorate for an energetic sense of fun.

Family rooms can often be noisy. Because too many hard surfaces will exaggerate sounds, tiled floors should be offset

Above: Using an old quilt maker's trick, a designer combined blocks of varied tonal depth to give a three-dimensional suggestion to the tile floor's faux-stone pattern.
Right: Practicality and dramatic sophistication come together in a floor that mixes contrasting perimeter tiles with reverse-pattern large-format squares. Both reappear combined as pieces in the jagged mosaic border for a faux-rug effect.

with plush draperies, soft furniture and pillows, rugs, and shelves of books. The family may gather in this room for watching TV or listening to music. A mix of hard and soft surfaces usually provides the best environment for pleasing sound quality.

Living and Dining Rooms. In some houses, the living room is truly the communal room, involving the considerations above. But when the floor plan allows for a separate family room, the living room usually becomes more of a company-only space and showcases the house's decorating approach, whether rugged, contemporary, neo-classically formal, country casual, or eclectic. Durability ratings become a less important consideration in less heavily trafficked rooms.

Dining rooms, too, tend

Above: To further enliven a kitchen garden room decorated with antique game boards, the owners opted for an equally graphic tile grid on the floor.

Right: A mosaic "hearth rug" is a showstopping work of art, yet the soft, hazy outlines and appealing natural tones keep it in scale.

to be company spaces, most often used for short, festive periods. Such rooms may be designed with a bit of lush theatricality, in deep reds and golds that look particularly good in low artificial light or candle glow. A tiled floor is practical wherever food is on the agenda. Unglazed tiles, unless impervious, should be sealed against grease and stains. The dining room needn't be quite as geared for heavy-duty use as the average kitchen; however, it might be just the spot for a colorful tiled "rug" to frame the table area or for bright inserts scattered in the field.

In many households, a little-used dining room takes on other duties, perhaps as a multipurpose room containing household files, a computer, or a sewing machine concealed in the credenza. In these rooms, where more time is spent, an easygoing neutral scheme may feel more appropriate.

Ways with Tile
Entryways, living and family rooms, sun rooms, bedrooms, fireplaces, wainscots, staircases, even furniture and accessories—all can be beautifully and durably finished in ceramics.

Below: A two-tone tile floor with a rustic glaze hews well to the simplicity and neutral color scheme in this hearthside dining area.

A WARM SPOT

Even in an era blessed with toasty central heating, the fire-place maintains its symbolic importance. It's also a time-tested spot for decorative tilework, more venerable than the modern kitchen or bath. Whether you're building a new fireplace or refacing an existing one, tile can make even a prefabricated, standard-issue unit more distinctive.

For safety, fireplace construction is strictly overseen by local building codes. The firebox is usually made of special, extremely heat-resistant firebrick, though it can also be clad with ceramic tile. The hearth, whether raised or level with the room's floor, is often tiled. Though all tile is nonflamma-ble and will shrug off sparks and soot, the hearth should be durable enough to withstand the scrapes of fire tools and the

Above right: Proper period fireplaces always presented a face of decorative tile.
Left: This fireplace's earth-toned tilework harks to the Arts and Crafts era, with its dimensional borders and ele-gant corner spandrels to shape the firebox arch.
Right: A turn-of-the-century room lightens up with sleek white-painted woodwork and glossy pillowed tiles.

Above: The hearth's strong form puts a clean edge on a lively mosaic.

Right: Lushly decorative, three-dimensional tilework creates a "fireplace" just for show.

impact of a heavy dropped log. Sealed vitreous quarry tiles, heavy-duty glazed floor tiles, or porcelain pavers are good candidates. Sometimes the hearth tile extends to a storage area for firewood and tools. In some large old houses, you might find a little seating niche there, romantically called an inglenook.

Tile struts its stuff more fully on the fireplace facing, where less-durable wall tiles will suffice, with their wide range of decorative possibilities. Fireplaces come in myriad styles. Tile

Above: Diamonds and squares in a rich matte glaze create the background for a nature-inspired hearth with frog-motif corner tiles and side panels of herons.

might cover wide panels framing the firebox, just form a narrow border, or ascend the chimney breast for a full-dress treatment. A row of tile can stand in for a conventional mantel, or jazz up a simple wooden shelf. If the mantel itself is a carved masterpiece, or it prominently displays collectibles and pictures, the tile background might be kept deliberately simple.

On a new fireplace, tile can be set into the wet mortar or plaster—an especially effective look for a stucco-covered, Southwestern fireplace. In Victorian times, iron fireplace inserts

were framed with "hearth sets" of tiles, displaying ascending murals of flowers or allegorical figures, the seasons, or biblical scenes. Arts and Crafts–era tiles were richly dimensional, often with lustrous glazes that glowed in firelight.

Tiled fireplaces require special heat-resistant mortars and grouts. To secure tiles to an existing masonry hearth, use cement-based products; over wood, metal, or existing tile, a heat-proof epoxy may be a more effective choice.

Above: A modern fireplace embodies a bit of Victorian splendor with high-relief tile designs under a deep-toned matte glaze.

Left: Simply wrapped in a minimalist mantel and tile in a warm tropical hue, a hearth exudes an exotically chic Art Deco air.

BRIGHT AND SUNNY SPACE

Above: Tile in large squares and simple crisscrossed bands carry the eye across the large conservatory, creating a floor that fits the scale of the space.

Whether you call it a greenhouse, solarium, conservatory, sun space, or sun room, such glassed-in rooms, open to the light and views, are favorite additions. A sun space can be planned as a place for growing plants, a passive collector for solar energy, or a year-round living space, but it's hard to design a space to meet all three aims without some compromises. Tile stars in all kinds of sun rooms because its durable, water-resistant surface is fade-proof, and the dense ceramic, installed over masonry, serves as "thermal mass" to moderate temperature swings and, thus, ensure more comfortable use of the space.

Solar Gain. Passive solar heating involves orienting your windows to within 30 degrees of due south to gather the low winter sun and building carefully planned overhangs to block high summer rays. A glass ceiling, though appealing for its skyward views, provides little warmth during the winter and contributes greatly to summer overheating. The thermal mass of floors and walls must be carefully determined for climate and exposure. Here's how it works: the floors and walls slowly absorb heat during the sunny hours of a winter day. When the air starts to cool during the early evening hours, the stored warmth is released. Many sun spaces are separated from the main house by insulated doors and are isolated when the temperatures drop at night and during gray days in winter to minimize the need for supplemental heating.

Floors and More. In a hot climate, you might be inclined toward a pastel floor that's brighter and cooler. (Solid-white floors are hard to keep clean with lots of outdoor-indoor traffic.) But in a chillier region, dark unglazed matte tile underfoot is more effective at gathering the sun's warmth. Sun spaces, like outdoor living areas, have to be decorated with sun-proof or easily replaceable fabrics and furnishings. So tile can serve a second function: to cover tables, shelves, benches, and cabinets in a setting that's hard on most other materials.

Below: In a sun room with a towering ceiling, a circle of cool-blue nonslip tile frames a welcoming indoor spa.

Sun spaces must be carefully tailored to the climate and the latitude to avoid summer overheating and to minimize the energy spent on heating and air-conditioning. For more information on sun rooms or incorporating passive solar principles into a new house's design, check out the consumer information provided by the Department of Energy's Energy Efficiency and Renewable Energy Clearinghouse (EREC) at 800-DOE-EREC (or 363-3732); www.eren.doe.gov/consumerinfo/. Your state energy-affairs commission is another good resource because it's attuned to local considerations.

A STEP ABOVE

Outdoors and in, stairways are graceful, rhythmic forms that lead the eye upward. Tile can add presence and grandeur to this feature, as it has for palaces and plazas throughout history.

Treads and Risers. The stair treads, where the foot lands, have to be no-nonsense—firm, even, and slip-resistant. Unglazed quarry and porcelain squares, or floor tiles with a gritty glazed surface, make a hard-wearing step. For extra grip, metal inserts with nonskid PVC treads can be added at the front edge. Special stair-tread tiles with rounded nosing protrude slightly over the riser to make a wider step on a steep stairway.

The risers can be more frivolous because durability isn't a prime concern, and a slick, glossy glaze makes it easier to remove an occasional scuff mark. All tiled risers may share one decorative tile, gaining impact from the repetition. Or each row may be different, but sharing a single theme or linked by similar colors. Often a highly decorative staircase takes its cue from a border or trim used on the first floor. Riser designs can be used to emphasize the horizontal or vertical to visually widen or heighten a run of stairs.

Opposite: In the Spanish tradition, a cascade of vibrant tile patterns draws the eye along the length of a grand central stairway. Brightly glazed risers alternate with nonslip, unglazed tile on the treads.

Above: Warm-toned terra-cotta makes a traditionally refreshing contrast with cooling shades of black. On this stairway, the repetition of the risers' pinstripe design emphasizes the long vertical flow.

Left: Despite their visual variety, these tiled risers share an old-world flavor that creates a unified whole.

Right: Designer Candace Bahouth lavishes her chapel studio with pattern, color, and her own artwork. One example is this mosaic column covered in bright ceramic shards.

Below: A more functional bit of ceramic artistry, a tiled side table is set on airy metal legs and edged with a delicately scrolled border.

OFF THE WALL

Not every tile installation is enduringly architectural. Tile can also adventurously finish a piece of furniture or stand as an artwork in its own right. Small ceramic flourishes are less of an investment, a way to showcase a tile you love but to which you can't commit for a major installation.

Furniture. In the eighteenth-century Rococo era, tile sometimes added details and medallions to fancy furniture. But it took the Victorian era's decorating verve to apply tile to tables, washstands, chairs, desks, buffets, pianos, and music stands. Today's homeowners still have all these options. A finish of tile can rejuvenate a tag-sale table or buffet, or conceal the simple plywood construction of a homemade bench or platform. For private spaces, tile could create a one-of-a-kind vanity table, nightstand, or hope chest.

Accent Pieces. Smaller accessories—lamp bases, picture frames, vases, planters, shelves, trays, and switch plates—can be dressed in tile, either with decorative squares or a newly composed mosaic. *Pique-assiette,* or "broken-dish," mosaic work incorporates random, broken bits of tile, sometimes mixed with other materials, into a free-form finish that can follow an object's shape. Such an approach uses leftover tiles, cut or broken after an installation.

Even single tiles set in wood frames make intriguing trivets and coasters for coffee cups or vases. Candles can be set on these heat-proof surfaces, secured with a drip of wax.

Above: A cheery tile patch-work runs from fireplace to a log-storage niche.
Right: Tiny mosaics can trace the curve of a vase.

Above: In a demonstration of the free-spirited nature of "pique-assiette," or "broken-dish," mosaic work, designer Kaffe Fassett's fireplace blends antique tiles with fragments of china in the same classic blue-and-white scheme.
Right: Multicolor mosaics give a tactile quality to a flat-topped column that Fassett designed to serve as a unique end table.

Opposite: A pair of glass-shelved display cases, lit from within, mass together an expanding collection of sculptural art tiles.
Left: To complete a colorful kitchen display of early twentieth-century pottery, a bright array of tiles from the same era marches across the top of the backsplash.
Below: A single fine example of antique tile, such as this detailed mosaic, can be framed and hung as artwork.

Collectibles. Antique tiles, whether Islamic, Dutch delft, French faience, or English or American "art tile," have become popular collectibles, with prices ratcheting ever higher. They deserve prominent display. Collected tiles can line up on a plate rail or on stands within a glassed-in breakfront. Individual tiles, mounted on wire-loop plate hangers, might deck the walls. Like any small artwork, they may need to be massed together for impact or placed individually in smaller nooks and odd bits of wall, rather than on the expanses.

Set on plate stands safely away from passing traffic, art tiles can create a display on a dresser or buffet. They can combine with other compatible collectibles or stand alone to command closer inspection. On the narrow ledge of a mantel or on an added molding at picture-rail height, special tiles can make a free-form border, the kind of decorative fillip that tile does so well.

CHAPTER 9

EXTERIOR TILE

Ceramics Under the Sun

While, today, we think of tile mainly as an interior dressing for our kitchen and baths, many of the most dazzling displays of ceramics throughout history have been al fresco, splashed with sunlight or water.

In fact, tile had its beginnings as an exterior flourish. From the colorful glazed brick of ancient Mesopotamia to the mosques of ancient Persia, gleaming in the Middle Eastern sun, to Spain's Moorish tiled courtyards and lavish fountains, and Italian villas with terra-cotta piazze and ceramic-clad columns—tile has often been where art meets nature.

Right: In nineteenth-century London suburbs, factory-made tile covered walkways with lively geometrics.
Below: Built in Spain, between 1904 and 1906, the apartment house Casa Battló, designed by architect Antonio Gaudí, has a tiled facade and roof.
Previous pages: Traditionally in sunny climes, shady courtyards are finished with mellow, earthy tiles.

In England and America, tile strayed outdoors during the Victorian era's revivals, alluding to classical or exotic styles, or adding another handmade touch to Arts and Crafts bungalows. In the expanding suburbs, English row houses boasted patchwork walkways, artistically composed with factory-made tiles in interlocking geometric shapes. And hand-painted tile panels flanking the front door were considered a refined touch, providing something of beauty for waiting visitors to contemplate.

Tile's history provides a jumping-off point for today's exterior applications. New varieties of ceramics and setting materials make tile practical outdoors in a wider climate range, whether for broad expanses of plazas and walkways or bright bits to trim a garden stairway or a house facade.

ARCHITECTURAL DRESSING

Tile adds character to a house's architectural face. Cities in Portugal are lavishly fronted with blue-and-white murals; in turn-of-the-century Vienna, an apartment house was tile-clad with Art Nouveau flowers twining from floor to floor. Nineteenth-century architects used easily cleaned, beautifully bright "faience" tilework to make ever-taller buildings more inviting at street level.

Although an increasing number of commercial buildings are clad in ceramic tile—sometimes dramatically decorative, sometimes evoking businesslike granite sheathing—such totally tiled facades are seldom seen in residential architecture. On the home front, exterior tilework more often provides handsomely individualistic detail, sometimes with site-specific pieces custom-made by tile artists. These might be a splendid arch of free-form mosaics to outline a window, a monumental ceramic frame on a doorway, or a decorative frieze fronting a portico. Or consider smaller, yet still effective, touches such as tiled house numbers, a tile-trimmed sidelight by the entry, decorative risers on the front steps, bright window boxes, or a ceramic "doormat."

GRACE NOTES: VICTORIAN DOORWAYS

The Victorians thought of everything—even as to how callers at their doorways might be entertained. Here are some spectacular examples to contemplate.

Right: Dating to the late-Victorian era, colorful, sculptural tiles by the Della Robbia Company in Berkenhead, England, appear as a frieze above a doorway in Hoylake.

Left: A late-Victorian doorway in Crewe, Cheshire, England, displays the era's tile.
Right: Nineteenth-century industry popularized finely detailed exterior tile-work. This panel is by the Photo Decorated Tile Company in Derby, England.

Tile seems particularly at home with Mediterranean- or Spanish-influenced buildings in stucco or adobe, perhaps topped with a classic red-tile roof. Ceramics are most easily applied to such masonry because other exterior finishes would first require an added underlayment, such as exterior-grade plywood or backer board. On a stucco house, ceramic accents can be adhered to the underlying "scratch coat" to sit flush with the smooth finishing layer, fashioning a bright inlaid design.

Above: Glazed tile is more vulnerable to weather extremes, and is often reserved for mild climates and vertical applications.

OUTDOOR DECORATING

However eye-catching tile can be as architectural accent, it commands more attention as part of an "outdoor room." It can run underfoot as an elegant patio or pathway, or trail up onto arches, fountains, pools, benches, barbecues, outdoor bars, and serving areas. It can brighten the risers of a stairway or add an ebullient mosaic or hand-painted mural to a bland retaining wall. It might serve as the showpiece of a tiny apartment balcony or as a subtle design detail seen throughout a country estate.

Opposite: Versatile ceramics extend from a rugged patio floor of unglazed pavers to a dynamically patterned outdoor hearth.

Above: Even a small dash of exterior tilework, such as a border below a threshold, can brighten a house's face.
Left: Tile applied to stucco's lower layer can fashion a handsome inlaid detail for doors and windows.

Opposite: Adding to the relaxed mood of an intimate little multilevel terrace is a mix of materials—stones, wood decking, and two different types of tile, including a free-form mosaic for the landing between the steps.

Above: With weather-resistant tile, an outdoor sitting area can be as stylish as any indoors. This chair and table, with their broken-tile mosaics and crisp checks edged in candy-bright trims, project an upbeat attitude.

The Outdoor Room. Current landscaping trends incline toward the "exterior decorating" of outdoor living spaces for a more furnished look and a definite sense of style. Outdoor casual furniture has become a booming, diversified product. You can buy an outdoor set in rugged Mission styling, neoclassic forms, postmodern funk, or romantic all-weather wicker. The outdoor spaces themselves are more likely to be defined with "verticals" of garden walls, trellises, decorative fountains, arches, and alcoves—all of which become more striking with tile. As an evocative, history-rich material, tile can instantly suggest an English cottage, a Japanese garden, a manor in Provence, a sultan's courtyard, or a Spanish palace.

Just as it does in a living room, exterior decorating starts with practicality and an assessment of the space itself. Is it a small, vest-pocket area that you want to unify with an easy sweep of low-key materials—or to enliven with a big punchy treatment? A truly tiny lawn is often better-used, more attractive, and easier to keep when it's paved over and set with container plantings. Or perhaps it's a rambling space you aim to divide visually into different functional areas, such as a dining corner, a children's play area, or a raised-bed garden. Combining tile with other compatible hard materials such as stone, slate, concrete, or decking, perhaps

with a change of levels, gives variety to a big blank space.

To emphasize its role as an extension of the house, the outdoor space may annex an indoor room of similar function—a dining patio off the dining room, a private terrace off the master suite. Because even simple foods seem festive when served and eaten outdoors, many exterior spaces lead off from the kitchen, handy for hosting a party or popping out for a few minutes with coffee and newspaper. Properly chosen, the same tile can run from inside to outside for a unified flow, though the effect grows less striking over the years as the exterior tile weathers. Even when not being used, an outdoor space "civilized" with tilework and seen beyond the windows can give a house an expansive feeling.

Sometimes, on a large property, the outdoor space is styled as a retreat, quite separate from the house, perhaps placed at the end of a pathway, obscured by trees, arbors, and vines. It may be so placed to gain a vista not seen from the house. In these cases, the tilework helps create a self-contained structure, perhaps framing the larger view and directing the eye, an approach referred to in descriptions of traditional Chinese gardens as "borrowing the landscape."

In the Garden

An avid gardener can incorporate tile into ongoing efforts, perhaps with a meandering path to lead the eye and the feet to favorite nooks among the greenery, or to provide a subtle background to brilliant seasonal hues. A bright border of tile puts a picture frame on a raised-bed garden and lends a spot of color to a wintry scene. If you're tepid about gardening, tile represents an object of beauty that doesn't need watering or mowing, and it can fill in the spaces between a few select plantings.

Floors and Walls. Multitalented tile extends easily between the horizontal and vertical. Tile can cover benches and planters, niches and dividers; mosaics might even follow the curves of large urns and columns. Resistant to heat and grease, tile can brighten a barbecue area and take part in a luxurious outdoor kitchen with wet bar and dining area and counters for preparing and serving food.

Archways and garden walls provide a large, prominent canvas for decorative, overall tile patterns, forming a background that completes the "outdoor room" illusion.

A recirculating wall fountain or a decorative ceramic plaque takes the design into bold relief.

Unglazed tiles are a classic paving material, giving a warmer, more-furnished look than poured concrete, albeit at considerably higher cost. New kinds of outdoor tiles are available, thinner, more compact and more colorful than the traditional heavy patio pavers. To lend variety to what might be a long, monotonous expanse, tiles of varied sizes and shapes can combine into attractive overall patterns, such as staggered squares, basket weave, or herringbone.

Plain pavers and quarries can also team up with more decorative tile inserted as an edging or scattered embellishment. Bright blues and green-blues, the complementary opposite to warm, earthy shades, are a time-honored choice for glazed outdoor accents. Borders and inserts serve, as they do inside, to provide a sense of movement and a separation of spaces while maintaining a visual link.

Above: What was once the barren cement of a tiny city courtyard gained a wrap-around rainbow of broken-tile mosaics, running from the paving up the wall.

Water Play.

Top: Exotic pheasants strut across a Moorish fountain of 1920s Malibu tiles.
Above: But even a smaller array of tile and water can be a garden's focal point.

Water Play. Water becomes even cooler, more playful and light catching in an outdoor setting when it's contained in colorful tile, whether a fountain or man-made waterfall, garden pond, spa, or an Olympic-size pool.

A fountain is an immediate centerpiece, creating an oasis with glittering movement and the gentle sound of water. This strong presence is enhanced by vivid tilework, perhaps a lively broken-tile mosaic or traditionally intricate whorls and arabesques of Spanish or Middle Eastern tradition, so vividly re-created in California's art tile of the 1920s and 1930s.

In swimming pools, glazed tile usually trims the waterline, though if budget permits it can extend across the cement bottom of the pool in striking designs. Some precast fiberglass pools are factory-fitted with a tile edging. Not only does the glossy tile emphasize the lapping movement of water but the glassy surface minimizes the whitish mineral deposits and scum left by evaporation. These are more noticeable on dark, decorative trim, and less so on the pale azure blue and turquoise tints popular for pools, which also mirror the coolness of the water and sky.

The coping, the nosed edge that juts out over the pool, may also be tiled, though cast-concrete is more customary. The decks and walkways around the pool must offer good traction and must slope slightly away from the pool to minimize puddles and prevent dirt from washing down into the water.

At Poolside

Pool tiles are often 6-inch squares but can vary from mosaics to large rectangles. While they commonly include useful lane markings and depth designations, pool trims can also circle the water with richly exotic patterns or bold geometric designs. Glass tiles add a special decorative shimmer. Most pool tile is made specifically for such applications, though other vitreous tiles, with an impervious glaze resistant to the chemicals, may be suitable as well.

Practical concerns are similar for spas and hot tubs, though their smaller size makes an all-over tile pattern more doable. In a deluxe setting offering both, the trim from the pool may extend into a more complete treatment for the spa. Spas and hot tubs can be installed in-ground or in a raised surround, similar to a bathroom's platform tub. Some are even free-standing. Such portable spas should not be set directly on a tiled patio, since its filled weight could crack the tiles.

PRACTICAL CHOICES

Not every tile can go outdoors successfully. Tiles used underfoot must be slip-resistant, particularly in areas around stairs or water. Unglazed tiles, pebbly mosaics, and glazed tiles with gritty or dimensional designs will usually fit that requirement.

In consistently dry, warm climates such as the Southwest, low-fired Mexican *saltillo* pavers and imported terra-cottas are often used outdoors. Even in mild conditions, the fairly soft tiles will show chips and wear, which may be acceptable as part of their rustic charm.

Tile, born of the fiery kilns, easily withstands heat and broiling sunlight, as demonstrated by its long association with the villas and haciendas of warmer climates. Technically, ceramics endure cold equally well. But only certain tiles can shift between the extremes. With a low-fired tile, water infiltrates the porous body and expands as it freezes, causing the tile to crack,

Above: For waterside tile, blue is a classically refreshing color choice. Here it shows its stylistic range, brightening both the old-world flowers and birds inset as panels in the stucco wall, and the modern, graphic tile stripes of the pool itself.

Above: Outdoor tile must be geared to the climate. Low-fired terra-cotta and glazed products won't withstand repeated freeze-thaw cycles. But in a warm climate, they add up to a time-tested look.

chip, and work loose—none of which happens with the denser body of a high-fired tile. In most climates, exterior tile must be vitreous enough to be billed as frost-proof by the manufacturer, usually with an absorption rate of 5 percent or less.

Vitreous quarry tiles and more costly impervious porcelain pavers, perhaps with a rusticated look, are durable, versatile choices. Some glazed products are also rated for outdoor use. Glazes are somewhat more vulnerable, particularly in horizontal applications where standing water might work into a hairline crack and craze the finish. Thus, exterior glazed tile facing a harsh climate must be highly vitrified. In milder climates, decorative and hand-painted tiles often appear on vertical features or as small accents inserted among more slip-resistant paving tiles.

ENDURING INSTALLATION

Choosing the proper tile is only part of the story. An equally important chapter is the installation. The mortar, adhesive, grout, and caulk must be specified for outdoor installation and to withstand temperature extremes.

Foundation. Tile pavements are usually thin-set on a concrete slab. An existing slab in reasonable condition can be tiled, after it's cleaned, patched and, if very smooth, roughened slightly for better adhesion. Major cracks and cleavages indicate inherent weakness in the concrete or an unstable subsurface—situations to remedy prior to tiling.

The concrete should be even, without dips, and sloped slightly for drainage, since standing water can undermine tile. If a slab collects rainwater, you may have a professional resurface it with a thick mortar bed, properly sloped with a drop of at least $1/8$ inch per foot. This allows any attached patio or walk to divert water away from the house's foundation, or a freestanding slab to shed water down from the center. Once the mortar cures, tiles can be applied with thin-set adhesives.

Tiled balconies and terraces should also have adequate drainage, lined underneath with a waterproof membrane to prevent water from seeping down to the spaces below.

Pouring Concrete. Pouring a new slab usually requires a building permit and inspections to ensure that the work meets local codes, which may vary slightly due to climate and soil conditions. If you've already chosen a tile, the new masonry can be sized to the tile's dimensions.

Concrete is poured over a sand-and-gravel base, dug out to the depth dictated by local conditions. The fresh concrete is cut with control or expansion joints. These localize any cracking within the crevice, where it's less obvious and readily repaired. These joints are spaced at a maximum of every 8 to 16 feet depending on the climate, the slab thickness, and the concrete mixture.

Mortar and Grout. When the tile layout is planned, grout spaces should end up directly over the control joints; those spaces should be filled not with grout, but with a compressible foam material and flexible outdoor-rated caulking. Such joints also allow for movement where tile changes level or meets another material, such as alongside a wall, column, or flagpole. Tinted and sanded caulks help blend in these joints, but they should still, whenever possible, be planned to fall unobtrusively in the overall design.

Ideally, cement-based mortars and grouts should be applied at moderate temperatures, out of the direct sun: excessive heat makes the cement dry too quickly before the maximum bond strength is achieved. After the installation has set and cured, unglazed tiles are often sealed to increase stain resistance and reduce water infiltration. But follow the tile manufacturer's recommendations, since some advise against sealing certain products. Right down to the final details, the careful choice of products and procedures helps assure that your outdoor tilework will take its place in a proud open-air tradition.

Top: Decorative tile fronts a planter in broken-tile mosaic and the stair risers in bright flowers, while an unglazed quarry tile makes a nonslip stair tread.
Above: The grout lines around smaller tiles also increase the traction underfoot. New steps and slabs can be sized to fit the tile's dimensions.

CHAPTER 10

LIVING WITH TILE

The Lowdown on Upkeep

One of ceramic tile's charms is that its beauty endures with a minimum of maintenance. Its smooth, nonabsorbent, nonstatic face gathers less grime than other surfaces under similar use, and the dirt that does gather is easily removed. You can further minimize your housekeeping with a little advance planning in choosing low-care tiles and installation materials. If maintenance is a special concern, discuss the specific care instructions for different products with a tile retailer.

PROTECTING NEW INSTALLATIONS

With newly mortared and grouted tilework, follow the manu-facturers' instructions regarding drying and curing times before subjecting the installation to foot traffic or heavy cleaning. Cement-based mortars and grouts continue to cure and gain strength and hardness throughout the first month. Whitish grout haze from cement-based grouts should be wiped with clear water and a clean sponge, and the tile face buffed with a dry cloth. Persistent grout haze may require a special remover, available from a tile retailer. Epoxy products are especially tough to remove once dry and must be carefully mopped up during installation.

SELECTING SEALERS

The glassy surface of a glazed tile is nonabsorbent and readily sloughs off dirt and splashes. High-fired vitreous quarry tiles and impervious porcelain tiles are similarly dense and nonab-sorbent. But many unglazed tiles are more vulnerable and should be sealed against moisture and stains in high-use areas and periodically resealed as recommended by the manufac-turer. Because polishing can open up microscopic pores in the tile surface, polished porcelains may need sealing in certain applications.

Sealers may be either surface coatings or penetrating prod-ucts. Either type can slightly change the tile's appearance, so test the proposed sealer on a sample first.

Surface coatings, often of acrylic or polyurethane, add a protective top layer for superior resistance to stains. It can also impart a surface sheen, which may or may not be to your taste. Every few years, when wear and scratches start to show, strip and reapply such coatings.

Penetrating sealers soak into the tile, possibly dark-ening it while adding a mellow protective patina that's not quite as protective as the hard top coat. Penetrating sealers need to be reapplied every few years but do not require stripping. An alternative method of sealing quarry tiles is to

cover the floor with an oil-based cleaner, full strength, and let it soak in for half an hour before wiping and washing. Repeat the procedure over several days until a desired patina is reached.

Cement-based grouts, after curing, should also be sealed, as recommended by the manufacturer. Penetrating silicone sealers are more water resistant than acrylics, which will suffice in less heavy-duty areas. Often, the grout lines and tiles are sealed simultaneously with a coating spread with a foam-rubber paint roller. Or more tediously, the sealant may be applied to the grout alone with a narrow brush.

After sealing, some unglazed quarry and terra-cotta tiles are treated with a tile wax, which may be tinted to enhance the earthy color. High-quality wax will endure a number of cleanings. After the floor is washed, rinsed, and dried, buffing will bring up the luster again. Wax must be stripped and reapplied when it no longer buffs satisfactorily.

PLANNING FOR EASY UPKEEP

As in any decorative material, very light or very dark choices demand more housekeeping (and a black-and-white checker-board floor, however jazzy it looks, shows everything). Think twice about dark, glossy tiles in a location subject to soapy splashes, makeup, and toothpaste drips. Lightly textured, patterned, or mottled surfaces in mid-tones or earthy hues are more concealing than flat solid colors. High-relief or carved-in intaglio designs can be dirt-trappers. An extremely slip-resistant floor tile, with a gritty glaze or incised patterns, similarly gives grime a better foothold.

Grout is usually more of a maintenance worry than the tile itself. Installing a large-format tile will reduce the number of grout lines. An even better strategy is selecting lower-maintenance products. A basic portland cement-based grout becomes more water- and stain-resistant and less prone to cracking when formulated with polymer or latex additives. For damp environments, consider a grout with mildew

Opposite: A solid grid of dark, bold color looks dramatic.
Above: Pure white tile may also demand some extra care, particularly in a kitchen, to keep its pristine appearance.
Previous pages: Luckily, ceramic's smooth, impervious surface is easy to clean, and suited for damp or high-use areas, such as shower stalls.

inhibitors. Even with performance-enhancing additives, most cementitious grouts should be sealed and periodically resealed. Such coatings are not required for the dense, smooth finish of epoxy grouts. Regardless of its formulation, a flat, narrow grout joint flush with the tile surface is generally the easiest to keep.

ROUTINE CARE

Low-tech preventive maintenance helps keep tile a no-fuss finish. Planning an adequate ventilation system into the design reduces mildew-forming dampness in bathrooms and greasy smoke residue in kitchens. Spills and splashes should be wiped up as they happen, and floors should be swept or vacuumed frequently to remove abrasive grit, particularly near exterior entrances. In shower stalls, towel-down or squeegee walls after use to keep moisture from fostering mildew.

Above: Water and mild detergent are usually sufficient to clean a tiled counter. A spray-on glass cleaner can bring up the shine on high-gloss tile.

For routine cleaning of glazed tiles and sealed unglazed squares, both floors and walls, damp-mop or sponge with hot water and a mild, neutral detergent—soaps leave a dulling film that can encourage mildew in wet areas. Rinse and wipe with a soft, dry cloth to finish the job. A spray-on window cleaner may be necessary for glossy tilework. Metallic or luster tiles, which tend to react with chemicals, may require a special metal cleaner. When swabbing dirty floors, change the water frequently, and rinse well to prevent residue in the grout lines. A mild vinegar solution may remove hard-water deposits in bath areas.

For heavier maintenance, such as renewing a grubby old tile installation, ask your tile dealer for specific cleaners, and use as directed after first testing in an unobtrusive spot. For grease and many other stains, a neutral household cleaner applied full strength and left to stand a few minutes before scrubbing and rinsing may be sufficient. You can scour grout lines with a nylon brush or a plastic pot scrubber, but avoid steel wool, which can leave embedded metal fibers and ensuing rust stains. Scrubbing tends to remove sealers, which should be reapplied.

Below: Mosaic tiles create an attractive visual texture and more grout lines to keep clean. Commercial cleaners are usually effective against mildew and stains. In wet areas, such as this tub surround, consider mildew-resistant grout formulas.

The traditional remedy for mildew is bleach, scrubbed on with a toothbrush. But be cautious of such aggressive treatments, as well as acidic or abrasive cleaners that can etch some glazes or mottle a tinted grout. A commercial mildew remover, tested in an inconspicuous spot, is usually effective, followed by ongoing preventive measures to keep mildew at bay. Persistent mildew problems might indicate moisture behind the wall, either from a slow plumbing leak or the failure of imperfect grouting, sealing, or caulking.

Specialty cleaners and stain removers may be caustic or toxic; pay careful attention to directions and precautions. Protect skin and eyes, and use in well-ventilated areas. Avoid mixing different cleaners, especially ammonia and bleach products, which combine to produce hazardous vapors.

Exterior tiled surfaces need only to be swept periodically and hosed down, and if necessary, scrubbed with mild detergent. Moisture wicking up through mortar and tiles can leave efflorescence, a whitish mineral residue, on the tile surface. If possible, reduce the moisture to minimize the problem. To remove the residue, scour the surface with a stiff-bristled brush and rinse. For stubborn efflorescence, ask your tile dealer about a sulfamic acid solution, which is swabbed onto wet tiles, scrubbed, and rinsed thoroughly.

OUT WITH THE OLD...

Broken or loosened tiles or cracked grout can be replaced. But first make sure that the crumbling grout or falling tiles aren't manifesting a larger hidden problem, such as excessive movement of the substrate or insidious water damage from behind. Such underlying problems need attention before spot repairs are made. Grout improperly mixed or cleaned too soon may be weak from the start.

Scrape out crumbly grout with a sharp awl, a narrow screwdriver, or a triangle-tipped can opener. Or speed the task with a job-specific grout saw. Scrub out the joints and vacuum to remove the debris before regrouting as directed.

To replace a loose wall tile, remove the surrounding grout, and gently pry out the tile with a wide putty knife. After scraping the dried adhesive from the tile and the wall, and patching and smoothing the underlayment, "back-butter" the tile with fresh adhesive, and press it into place. Remove any excess adhesive while it's wet. Tape the tile in place with spacers alongside, and tamp it flat with its neighboring tiles with a cloth-covered block of wood. Allow adhesive to cure before grouting.

The procedure is similar for replacing a damaged tile. Remove the surrounding grout, score the damaged piece with a glass cutter, and chisel out. Hold the chisel at a low angle to avoid gouging the substrate, and tap gently with a hammer to avoid damaging adjoining tiles. Tile shards can be as sharp as glass, so wear eye protection when removing old tile.

PLANNING FOR SUCCESS

Tilework Planner

Rigid, modular tile is unyielding in its demands for a well-planned layout and proper installation. When you're envisioning your house decked out in ceramic tile, certain practicalities intrude on the picture. If you're considering installing your own tile, you should have these practicalities firmly in hand. Many uncomplicated residential tile projects are within the grasp of the motivated do-it-yourselfer armed with complete directions and a methodical approach. Even if you're hiring a professional installer, understanding tile's practical demands, as discussed in this planner, will help you plan your project and communicate with your installer more effectively.

Left: If both floors and walls are tiled, it can be tricky to precisely align the grout joints, so often different size tiles are chosen for each.

INSTALLATION MATTERS

Tile is only a pretty face. To be a durable surface, it must be backed up with a sturdy underlying surface and appropriate setting materials. Failed tilework more often is traced to problematic installation than to a fault with the material itself.

In centuries past, tile was often applied to massive masonry surfaces—cathedrals, mosques, and castles. Today, the common problem is wedding a rigid ceramic square to a springier wood-framed house. An installer's first step is assessing the underlying structure, sometimes in consultation with a structural engineer. Not only must the framework bear the weight of tile and installation materials but it also must not flex unduly under the load. Flexible installation materials and isolation joints can adapt tile to a somewhat "lively" structure. But a floor that gives under weight more than $\frac{1}{8}$ inch in a 10-foot span, according to the Tile Council of America (TCA), should be reinforced to avoid cracked and popped tiles. Or, in certain cases, a professional may install a "floating floor" that isolates the tile installation from the structural movement.

For vertical tile applications, load-bearing walls are generally sturdy enough for any tilework. But if a project calls for a non-load-bearing partition wall to be tiled, it may need an added joist constructed underneath it to support a heavy installation.

METHODS

Prior to the 1950s, tile was laid into a thick layer of mortar, reinforced with metal lath. Since then, such thick-bed or mud-set methods have taken second place to thin-bed or thinset installation, which bonds the tile to a surface with a thin layer of mortar or adhesive.

The thick mortar bed still has advantages: it can true-up an uneven surface and create accurate slopes and curves. The results are structurally rock-solid and water-resistant. Today, instead of setting tiles into the wet mortar, an installer will often "float" a mortar bed, allow it to dry, and then set the tiles over it with thinset methods. On the downside, the thick-bed approach is more expensive and time-consuming, and requires an experienced installer. It also adds weight—as much as 20 pounds per square foot—and raises the floor height by as much as 2 inches.

Thinset installation has taken the lead because it's easier, faster, less expensive, and less massive. One trade-off: for the thin layer of mortar or adhesive to bond effectively, the underlying surface, or substrate, must be clean, rigid and flat within $\frac{1}{8}$ inch over 10 feet. Preparing the surface, or covering it with an appropriate underlayment, is crucial to success.

ADHESIVES

Thinset adhesives span a wide, changing, and sometimes confusing category of products. The tile dealer can help the do-it-yourselfer sort through and match the adhesive to the site conditions, the chosen tile, and the substrate. Manufacturers of installation materials will also answer technical questions. Select well-known brands, certified by the major tile trade organizations.

Tile-setting adhesives come in three families: portland-cement-based mortars, organic mastics, or epoxies.

Portland cement mortar is the broadest category, with myriad formulations geared to specific substrates, to certain levels of dampness or temperature, or for thicker application with irregular handmade tile. Some are ready-to-use, but most are powdered, to be mixed on-site.

Portland cement gains strength when it dries slowly. Traditionally, tiles have been soaked prior to setting, and the new installation is kept damp to slow the curing. Dry-set mortars contain an additive that retains water, so tiles can be set dry. Another common additive is a powdered polymer included in the mix, or a liquid latex used in place of water. Either makes the bond stronger, denser, and more water-resistant, with latex having the edge. Properly chosen, cement mortars can work on most substrates and will fill in some minor surface irregularities.

Organic mastics (so dubbed because they were originally made from natural rubber) are premixed adhesive pastes, based on latex or petrochemicals. A favorite with do-it-yourselfers, mastics are less expensive

Here's a rundown of some common substrates:

◆ **Concrete and masonry** make an excellent base if dry, completely cured, flat, and uncracked; a self-leveling compound can fix some minor defects. If drops of water bead up on the concrete, it was treated with a drying agent that should be sanded or water-blasted off, as it will interfere with some mortars.

◆ **Drywall or cured plaster**, if sound and smooth, can serve as a tile substrate in a dry location. Wallpaper should be removed and paint scarified. Moisture-resistant wallboard, also called greenboard or blueboard, is better for damp conditions, though it will not bear up to constant wetness. Using portland-cement-based backer board in wet areas instead of greenboard or blueboard is recommended.

◆ **Existing tile** is acceptable only if firmly attached and flat—don't be tempted to hide suspected water damage or structural problems. The old tile should be cleaned and roughened to give the adhesive a good grip. Unsound tilework should be pulled out—no easy task, particularly in an old thick-bed installation. Tile shards are sharp, so demolition calls for eye protection, heavy clothing, and a respirator face mask. Shield the tub or shower pan from falling tile with layers of heavy cardboard and a tarp.

◆ **Laminate counters**, if sturdy and unwarped, can be tiled over, after an initial roughening.

◆ **Resilient flooring** must be solid, flat, and not too resilient, because tiles laid on soft, cushioned vinyl can crack. Glossy surfaces should be degreased and sanded. A word of caution: resilient floors installed prior to 1985 may contain asbestos fibers, which can be hazardous if released into the air. These floors should not be sanded, scraped, or torn. Unless you want to have a sample tested, assume an old resilient floor contains asbestos. If it's not firm enough to tile directly, cover it with plywood or backer board. Or check on removal and disposal guidelines from your local Environmental Protection Agency office or the Resilient Floor Covering Institute, Rockville, MD; (301) 340-8580, [www.rfci.com/tech.html].

◆ **Plywood** is a traditional tile underlayment. To minimize the possibility of water damage, use exterior-grade products, and check that each sheet is flat and smooth. Interior-grade plywood and composite products such as particleboard are too vulnerable to moisture—and plank floors too uneven—to serve as a tile backing without an added layer of plywood.

◆ **Backer board**, made specifically for tile, can either be portland-cement-based panels, which need to be cut with a saw, or lighter-weight panels of cement sandwiched with fiberglass mesh, which can be scored and snapped. Though more expensive, backer board is often the substrate of choice because it is stable, water-resistant, and stays rigid when wet. Like wallboard, backer board is available in various thicknesses and is attached to studs or plywood backing with galvanized screws. For flooring, backer board needs a plywood support set over joists to bear weight.

and are easy to work with because they're ready-to-use and smooth-spreading. Though mastics are not as strong as cement-based mortars, they can serve well for dry areas and low-use floors. Mastics don't flow to fill gaps, so they require a particularly smooth and completely dry underlayment.

Epoxy mortars, just like familiar epoxy glues, include a separate resin and hardener to be mixed with a filler such as silica sand. Epoxies are more expensive and harder to use because they must be mixed with precision and applied promptly at the right temperatures and

Tile's exacting geometry often has to reconcile with a less-than-perfect room. Part of the initial structural assessment is determining how close the floors and walls come to being perfectly square and true. Small deviations are accommodated by trimming the end tiles at a slight angle. Serious problems may involve some rebuilding of the floors or walls with shims to bring the new backing into line.

Renovators are forced to cope with such existing conditions. But in new construction, you can prevent tile installation headaches by specifying in the contract that the intended site to be tiled should meet construction guidelines stated in the Tile Council of America's "Handbook for Ceramic Tile Installation."

In laying out the tiles themselves, an experienced tile setter might simply order the requisite square footage of tile and finesse during the installation some of the finer points of a graceful arrangement. But a novice may want to first map out on paper how the tile will fit the space. This starts with a scale drawing of the wall or floor on graph paper, with careful note of cabinets, windows, door-ways, and architectural features. But the basic measuring unit is not feet or inches: each square represents the actual size of the tile (which may differ from its nominal size) plus one grout line. Tracing-paper overlays can be used to try out different configurations and to plan the placement, sketched in with colored pencils, of any multicolor designs, borders, or murals.

Ideally, the layout will gracefully frame the room's most prominent features: if a window, door or fireplace can't be flanked in full tiles, the cut tiles to either side should be the same width so the feature appears centered. Cut tiles should be unobtrusive, and symmetrical on both sides of the room. If the first plan ends up with a narrow row of cut tiles along one wall, widening the grout lines slightly all across the floor may eliminate it. (Narrow slivers of tile not only look awkward, they're more likely to work loose.) Or the whole row can be shifted to end up with similar wider-cut tiles on opposite walls. Real-life layouts often involve compromises: for example, centering the tile at the windows may result in cut-tiles along only one wall.

with good ventilation. They're often tapped for commercial installations that require epoxy's high level of bond strength and resistance to chemicals and impact. Certain epoxies are heat-resistant, for use around range hoods, woodstoves, and grills. Epoxies bond well with just about any substrate, including metals and existing tiles.

Furan adhesives and grouts are resin-based, like epoxies, but are generally reserved for industrial settings, which are subject to heat, chemicals, and heavy loads.

GROUT

Grout is mortar forced into the spaces between the tiles to fill the gaps, protect the edges, and stem water infiltration. It comes in assorted formulations geared for certain types of tile and particular conditions with most based either on portland cement or epoxy.

Cement-based grouts, more commonly used, generally come in powdered form, often with water-retaining dry-set additives. Powdered polymers or liquid latex may be added for a more resilient, water-resistant joint, with latex formulations generally more resistant to chemicals and impact. For joints wider than $\frac{1}{16}$-inch, sand is added to strengthen the material and cut shrinkage. Once completely cured, cement-based grouts, are generally topped with an acrylic, lacquer, or silicone sealer, as recommended by the manufacturer, to fend off stains and water infiltration.

Epoxy grouts resist water, stains, chemicals, and mildew, and require no sealing, which makes them a good choice for kitchens. They are, however,

But planning ahead allows you to weigh the options.

The scale drawings guide the eventual installation, which begins with the laying down of the working lines. These are chalk lines, snapped on a floor or wall to keep the first row of tiles perfectly straight, particularly if adjustments are being made for the room's vagaries. Wooden battens are attached along these lines so that the tiles can be butted against the firm, straight edge.

Wall tiles are installed from the bottom up. The horizontal working line, rigorously level, is often placed one row up from the bottom, with the accompanying batten to support the work. After the tiles are set, the batten is removed, the bottom row of tiles inserted.

Floors may be tiled outward from the center, one quadrant at a time, starting from working lines that cross at the center in a perfect 90-degree angle, oriented to the primary wall, often the one facing the entrance. This works well if there's a central decorative motif, or if adjustments will be made along all four walls in a room badly out of square. If the tile design is unvaried, and at least two corners of the room are square, many installers snap the working lines and begin laying tile starting at one wall.

The tiles, with spacers, are usually laid out along the working lines in a dry run to double-check the layout. If necessary, working lines can be shifted to adjust the size of the cut tiles. For tiles with lots of color variation, the dry run also assures a graceful flow of shifting tones.

If both floors and walls are tiled, it can be tricky to precisely align the grout joints, so often different size tiles are chosen for each. Generally the tile with greater visual weight, such as the larger square or the strong pattern of a mosaic, goes underfoot. Walls are usually installed first to minimize the activity on a newly laid floor.

To cut thin wall tiles and many glazed floor tiles score and snap them with an ordinary glass cutter or a snap-cutter tool. Tile nippers create irregular or curved cuts to fit around pipes and fixtures. Cutting heavy-duty floor tiles may require a wet saw, also available for rent. Or a do-it-yourselfer can mark the cuts needed and have them done by the tile dealer.

more expensive and more difficult to apply. Safety precautions on the package should be followed carefully. With its thick consistency, epoxy won't flow to fill a wide grout joint. Careful clean-up is essential—epoxy grout inadvertently dried on the tile surface is tough to remove. Its smooth, dense finish may look too slick to suit a rustic-looking tile.

Grout is firmly rubbed across the surface of the set tiles and packed into the joints with a rubber-faced trowel called a float. With very rough, dimensional tile, the grout may be delivered directly into the joints with a grout bag to minimize grout on the tile, which would be difficult to clean. As the grout firms up, the excess is wiped away with a damp sponge and the joints more firmly pressed and shaped with a "striking" tool. When the grout dries, the tile faces are again cleaned and polished with a dry cloth. The installation should be protected while the grout hardens over two to seven days, though the cement grouts gain strength through the first month.

Grouts are now available in hundreds of colors. A boldly contrasting color plays up the grid pattern, while a closely matched choice makes the installation more monolithic. A natural grayish cement color is neutral and unobtrusive, and darker shades are more practical underfoot. The dyes of a strongly tinted grout may bleed into an unglazed tile, which may need to be sealed beforehand.

Flexible caulk, which adapts to movement, is used to fill the joint when tilework changes plane, such as

HIRING A PRO

Because installation is crucial, seeking out a tile contractor who's a true professional is worth the time. Tile installers, unlike electricians or plumbers, do not undergo formal apprenticeships and licensing procedures. While tile contractors are listed in the Yellow Pages, a word-of-mouth recommendation from friends, neighbors, or co-workers is often the better start. Your architect, designer, or general contractor probably can vouch for certain local firms.

Large tile showrooms may have on-staff installation crews, or a representative may be able to make a recommendation. Trade organizations, such as the Ceramic Tile Institute of America and the National Tile Contractors Association, may also refer you to local members.

When you've assembled a short list, ask each contractor for a list of references so that you can talk to former clients. If possible, try to see some of their work rather than relying on someone else's assessment. Does the project make a good overall impression? Then look at the details: Are the patterns gracefully and symmetrically placed, with special regard for the sight lines on entering the room? Are grout lines straight and even, and corners neatly turned? Are the cut tiles placed unobtrusively, and the layout adjusted to avoid thin slivers of tile along one edge? It's more revealing to look at an installation that's a few years old, when any problems such as loose or cracking tiles or grout may have emerged.

Installation costs vary widely, depending on the region and the job's complexity. Cost per square foot is lowest for a straightforward flat floor consisting of the same tile, and soars for a small project with lots of precisely cut tiles and details. Irregular handmade tile may also be more time-consuming to install. If you've visualized something particularly special, you may be looking for an installer who's also a bit of an artist.

Get at least three bids, based on the same materials and methods, so they're truly comparable. Fight the natural urge to jump for the low bid, unless you can choose with confidence. You want an installer who would, for example, suggest beefing up the sub-floor so the tiles stay put, rather than someone who would skip that step to offer a low price.

The chosen tile contractor should be properly insured, so you're not liable for worker accidents on your property. He or she should be willing to draw up a detailed contract, spelling out any preliminary surface preparation, and the exact installation materials and methods. Work should be specified as meeting local building codes and TCA installation guidelines. Such precautions better the chances that your tile installation will live up to its potential.

---

a sink or toilet. Caulks are now blended to match grouts to make such seams unobtrusive, and may be sanded for a similar texture. Caulk requires periodic replacement, particularly at the tub-line joint, which is stressed when the tub is filled and emptied.

Though many mortars, grouts, and sealers are formulated to be water-resistant, none can be guaranteed to be waterproof—moisture is insidious and can work its way into underlayment over time. Wet conditions call for a moisture barrier applied over the wall studs. A waterproof membrane, such as a fiberglass mesh brushed with a light tar, can be applied over the backing before the tile is applied. Make sure that any waterproofing methods are compatible with the intended underlayment and mortar, and meet local building codes.

GLOSSARY

Absorbency Rating: Industry measure of how much water a tile will absorb, as a percentage of its weight, indicating the density of the clay body. Also referred to as "porosity."

Backer Board: Portland-cement-based panel specifically used as a water-resistant, dimensionally stable underlayment in thinset tile installation.

Bicottura: Italian for "twice fired." Refers to decorative tiles that are fired to harden the green clay into bisque, then fired again to fuse the glaze and any decoration.

Bisque: Fired, unglazed clay body, also called biscuit or bisquit.

Bullnose: Trim tile with a rounded edge.

Clays: Fine-grained earthy material, based on aluminum silicates, which are malleable when wet, rigid when dried, and permanently hard when fired.

Cove Tile: Trim piece that smoothly rounds out a 90-degree inside or outside corner.

Crazing: Fine cracks spreading across a glazed surface under stress, sometimes intentionally created to suggest an aged appearance.

Curing: Chemical change over time, through which mortars and grouts dry and gain strength.

Dust-Pressing: Tile production process that shapes almost-dry clay in high-pressure molds.

Expansion Joint: In a tile installation, a joint filled with flexible material to allow for slight movement where floor meets wall, or the tile abuts another material.

Extrusion: Tile production process where moist clay is pressed through a die and sliced into squares or rectangles.

Glaze: A protective, decorative glassy finish, colored with metallic oxides and chemically bonded to a ceramic surface by the kiln's heat.

Grout: Mortar that fills the spaces between installed tiles. A binder and filler applied in the joints between ceramic tile.

Impervious Tile: High-fired, vitrified tiles with absorption levels below 0.5 percent, sometimes referred to as porcelain.

Majolica (or Maiolica): Loose term for earthenware tile covered with white tin glaze and decorative painting, or, occasionally, for relief-molded tiles with glossy glaze.

Mastic: Premixed thinset tile adhesive that has a latex or petrochemical base.

Monocottura: Italian for "single-fired." Refers to tiles fired once to harden the raw clay and fuse the glaze.

Mortar: Mixture of portland cement, sand, and water spread in heavy layer to underlay a thick-set installation. More loosely, the cement-based or epoxy adhesives that bond tile to the work surface in a thinset installation.

Mosaic: Industry term for tile smaller than 2.4 inches by 2.4 inches.

Mud Bed: See Thick Bed.

Nonvitreous Tile: Low-fired, porous tiles with absorption rates above 7 percent.

Paver: Loosely, any tile shaped by molding, whether low-fired terra-cotta or impervious porcelain.

Porosity: See Absorbency Rating

Porcelain: See Impervious Tile.

Quarry Tile: Extruded vitreous or semivitreous floor tiles, usually unglazed and red bodied.

Sealer: Liquid coating to protect unglazed tiles and grout.

Semivitreous Tile: Fairly high-fired tile, with a water-absorbency rating between 3 and 7 percent. Some tiles in this range are frost proof.

Terra-cotta: Loose term for molded nonvitreous or semivitreous unglazed tiles often of a reddish color and commonly imported.

Thick Bed: Tile installation method that lays tile on a mortar bed of more than 1/2 inch. Also called a mud bed or thickset.

Thinset: Tile installation method that bonds tiles to a substrate with a thin layer of mortar or adhesive.

Underlayment: Plywood or backer-board panels laid as a smooth base for setting tile.

Vitreous Tile: High-fired, frost-proof tile with a water absorbency rating between 0.5 and 3 percent.

Index

Photography Credits

p. 1 Superstock. p. 2 Tony Giammarino. p. 8 www.davidduncanlivingston.com. p. 9 left to right Moravian Tile Works, Superstock. pp. 10-11 left to right Tony Arruza/Bruce Coleman, Inc., Christie's Images. pp. 12-13 left to right J.C. Carton/ Carto/Bruce Coleman, Inc., Superstock, Inc., Mary Zisk. p. 14 F. Jack Jackson/ Bruce Coleman, Inc. p. 15 top Christie's Images, bottom Superstock, Inc. p. 16 Christie's Images. p. 17 both Hans van Lemmen. p. 18 top left and right Hans van Lemmen, bottom left Mary Zisk. p. 19 Hans van Lemmen. p. 20 Hans van Lemmen. p. 21 Hans van Lemmen. p. 22 both Hans van Lemmen. p. 23 Stephen Saks/ Bruce Coleman, Inc. pp. 24-25 H& R Johnson Tiles. p. 26 National Archives. p. 27 left and center Erie Art Museum, right top, center, and bottom Tile Heritage Foundation. p. 28 all Moravian Tile Works. p. 29 left and top right Christie's Images, right bottom Tile Heritage Foundation. p. 30 left Perrault-Rago Gallery, right Tile Heritage Foundation. p. 31 left www.davidduncanlivingston.com, right top and bottom Tile Heritage Foundation. p. 32 Tim Street-Porter. p. 33 top Tile Heritage Foundation, bottom Perrault-Rago Gallery. p. 34 left top and bottom Tile Heritage Foundation, right top Christie's Images. p. 35 both Perrault-Rago Gallery. p. 36 both Tile Heritage Foundation. p. 37 Moravian Tile Works pp. 38-39 Mark Samu/ Gallo Kitchen. p. 40 top Abbate Tile, bottom Mark Samu. p. 41 Mark Samu; design: Ken Kelly. p. 42 Tony Giammarino. p. 43 Jessie Walker. p. 44 www.davidduncanlivingston.com. p. 45 Mark Samu. pp. 46-47 left to right Mark Lohman, Beth Singer. p. 48 Mark Samu. p. 49 Tony Giammarino. p. 50 Mark Samu. p. 51 www.davidduncanlivingston.com.pp. 52-53 www.davidduncanlivingston.com. p. 54 top Joan Gardiner, bottom Jessie Walker. p. 55 Tria Giovan. p. 56 Mark Samu. p. 57 top Ellie Stein, bottom www.davidduncanlivingston.com. p. 58 top Peter King, bottom K. Koblitz. p. 59 all Motawi Tile Works. pp. 60-61 left to right Peter Truitt, www.davidduncanlivingston.com, Mark Samu. p. 62 left to right Ellie Stein, Jessie Walker, www.davidduncanlivingston.com. p. 63 all Leo Peck. p. 64 www.davidduncanlivingston.com. p. 65 top RH & James Stonebraker, bottom Melabee M Miller pp. 66-67 Jessie Walker Associates. p. 68 Jessie Walker. p. 69 Photography: Peter Paige; Designer: Mark Polo. p. 70 Jessie Walker. p. 71 Rob Melnychuk. p. 72 Jessie Walker. p. 73 Jessie Walker. p. 74 top Brian Vanden Brink, bottom www.davidduncanlivingston.com. p. 75 Mark Samu. p. 76 top www.davidduncanlivingston.com, bottom Mark Lohman. p. 77 www.davidduncanlivingston.com. p. 78 all David Phelps. p. 79 top Janet Henderson, bottom Holly Stickley. p. 80 www.davidduncanlivingston.com. p. 81 Mark Samu. p. 82 Mark Lohman. p. 83 Mark Lohman. pp. 84-85 Mark Lohman. p. 86 Melabee M Miller; design: Crossville Tile. p. 87 Mark Samu; design: Ken Kelly. p. 88 Jessie Walker. p. 89 top Photography: Melabee M Miller; design: Tracey Stephens, bottom: Nancy Hill; design: Kitchens by Deanne. p. 90 top www.davidduncanlivingston.com, bottom photography: Mark Samu. p. 91 both Mark Samu. pp. 92-93 Gross & Daley. p. 94 both Jessie Walker. p. 95 Andrew McKinney. p. 96 Andrew McKinney. p. 97 Jessie Walker. pp. 98-99 left to right Tony Giammarino, Holly Stickley. p. 100 Mark Lohman. p. 101 all Jessie Walker. pp. 102-103. Mark Samu. p. 104 Photography: Mark Lohman; design: Cynthia Marks/ Ann Sacks Tile. p. 105 Melabee M Miller. p. 106 Phillip Thompson Photography. p. 107 left W. Day, right Jessie Walker. p. 108 left Jessie Walker, right Tony Giammarino. p. 109 Gross & Daley. p. 110 Tony Giammarino. p. 111 Tim Street-Porter. p. 112 top Rob Melnychuk, bottom Photography: Mark Samu. pp. 113-115 Mark Lohman. p. 116 left top and bottom Mark Lohman, right David Phelps. pp. 117-119 Mark Lohman. p. 120-121 Brian Vanden Brink. p. 122 Holly Stickley p. 123 left to right Mark Samu, www.davidduncanlivingston.com. pp. 124-125 Grey Crawford. pp. 126-127 left to right Tim Street-Porter, www.davidduncanlivingston.com, Beth Singer. pp. 128-129 left to right Jessie Walker, Holly Stickley, Mark Samu. p. 130 Holly Stickley. p. 131 top to bottom Janet Henderson, Mark Samu. p. 132 Tim Street-Porter. p. 133 www.davidduncanlivingston.com. p. 134 Holly Stickley. p. 135 top to bottom Holly Stickley, Gross & Daley. p. 136 www.davidduncanlivingston.com. p. 137 Superstock. p. 138 Grey Crawford. p. 139 top to bottom Holly Stickley, Tim Street-Porter. p. 140 top to bottom Hugh Burden/Period House Magazine, David Phelps. p. 141 clockwise from top left www.davidduncanlivingston.com, Rob Melnychuk, www.davidduncanlivingston.com, www.davidduncanlivingston.com. p. 142 www.davidduncanlivingston.com. p. 143 top to bottom Brian Vanden Brink , Christie's Images/Superstock. pp. 144-145 Tim Street-Porter. p. 146 top Nancy Hill, bottom Georg Gerster/ Photo Researchers. p. 147 all Hans van Lemmen. p. 148 left top Mark Lohman, left bottom Nancy Hill, right Robin Jane Solvang/ Bruce Coleman, Inc. pp. 149-152 Tim Street-Porter. p. 153 Oscar Paisley/ Period Homes Magazine. pp. 154-155 all Tim Street-Porter. p. 156 Grey Crawford. p. 157 top Nancy Hill, bottom Tim Street-Porter. pp. 158-159 Rob Melnychuk. pp. 160-161 left to right Brian Vanden Brink, Andrew McKinney. p. 162 Tria Giovan. p. 163 Mark Samu. p. 164 www.davidduncanlivingston.com.

Have a home decorating, improvement, or gardening project? Look for these and other fine Creative Homeowner books wherever books are sold. .

Projects to personalize your rooms with paint and paper. 300 color photos. 176 pp.; 9"×10"
BOOK #: 279723

p. 1

Learn how to make the most of color. More than 150 color photos. 176 pp.; 9"×10"
BOOK #: 287264

How to create kitchen style like a pro. Over 150 color photos. 176 pp.; 9"×10"
BOOK #: 279935

How to work with space, color, pattern, texture. Over 300 color photos. 256 pp.; 9"×10"
BOOK #: 279667

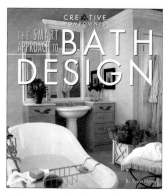

All you need to know about designing a bath. Over 150 color photos. 176 pp.; 9"×10"
BOOK #: 287225

Get the practical information you need to choose window treatments. Over 100 illustrations & 125 photos. 176 pp., 9"×10"
BOOK #: 279431

Turn an ordinary room into a masterpiece with decorative faux finishes. Over 40 techniques & 300 photos. 272 pp.; 9"×10"
BOOK #: 279550

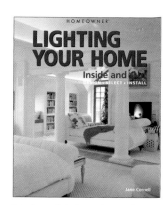

Design a lighting scheme for every room in your home and outdoors. 525 illustrations. 176 pp., 8^1/$_2$"×10^7/$_8$"
BOOK #: 277583

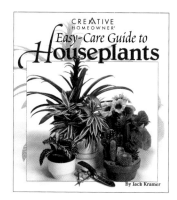

Complete houseplant guide. 200 readily available plants; more than 400 photos. 192 pp.; 9"×10"
BOOK #: 275243

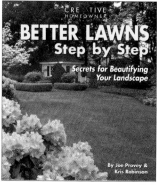

Create more beautiful, healthier, lower-maintenance lawns. Over 300 illustrations. 160 pp.; 9"×10"
BOOK #: 274359

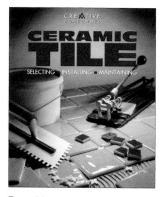

Everything you need to know about setting ceramic tile. Over 450 Photos. 160 pp.; 8^1/$_2$"×10^7/$_8$"
BOOK #: 277524

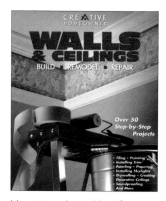

How to replace old surfaces with new ones. Over 450 illustrations. 160 pp.; 8^1/$_2$"×10^7/$_8$"
BOOK #: 277708

For more information, and to order direct, call 800-631-7795; in New Jersey, 201-934-7100.
Please visit our Web site at www.creativehomeowner.com